Motorbooks International

WARBIRD HISTORY

LOCKHEED
F-104
STARFIGHTER

Steve Pace

In memory of Kelly Johnson.

First published in 1992 by Motorbooks International Publishers & Wholesalers, PO Box 2, 729 Prospect Avenue, Osceola, WI 54020 USA

Motorbooks International books are also available at discounts in bulk quantity for industrial or sales-promotional use. For details write to Special Sales Manager at the Publisher's address

Library of Congress Cataloging-in-Publication Data
Pace, Steve.
    Lockheed F-104 Starfighter / Steve Pace.
       p. cm. -(Warbird History Series)
    Includes index.
    ISBN 0-87938-608-8
    1. Starfighter (Fighter plane)   I. Title.
    II. Series.
UG1242.F5   1992
358.4'382—dc20   92-9010

Printed and bound in Hong Kong

On the front cover: *US Air Force F-104A 56-736 climbs unencumbered by wingtip tanks or missiles. Lockheed via Eric Schulzinger*

On the frontispiece: *German air force F-104G blasts off on the first of many secret F-104 zero-length launch tests. Lockheed*

On the title page: *First of sixteen production F-104A-10 Starfighters parked on ramp at the Air Force Flight Test Center, Edwards Air Force Base (AFB), California, circa 1958. Aerospace Defense Command grey paint scheme is noteworthy; the aircraft was named* 'Lil Grey Dolphin *by USAF flight-test and evaluation crew. USAF*

On the back cover: *The F-104 Starfighter served with the US Air Force and fourteen allied air forces. Top, a Royal Canadian Air Force CF-104. Lockheed. Center, a Japanese Air Self-Defense Force F-104J. Lockheed. Bottom, this Luftwaffe F-104G of JBG 34 is specially painted in celebration of the group's twenty-fifth anniversary of flying the Starfighter. Arnold Booy via Gary James Collection*

Contents

Acknowledgments

I would like to thank the following for their help: Tony LeVier, Lockheed, retired; Ben Rich, Lockheed, retired; Eric Schulzinger, Richard Stadler, Denny Lombard, Roy Blay, T. G. Crawford, and April McKettrick of Lockheed Corporation; Cheryl Gumm, Dr. Jim Young, and Phil Tucker of the US Air Force Flight Test Center History Office; Rick Kennedy of General Electric Aircraft Engines; Don Nolan and Don Haley, NASA Public Affairs at Ames/ Dryden Flight Research Facility; Chris Wamsley, Rockwell International; Dr. Ira Chart, Northrop Corporation; Bob Hirsch; Robert F. Dorr; Marty Isham; Bert Kinsey, Detail and Scale; Dana Bell; Gary James; Dave Menard; John and Donna Campbell (Campbell Archives); Toni LeVier; Tom Rosquin (Thomas Aviation); James C. Goodall; Warren Thompson; Greg Field, aviation editor, Barbara Harold, managing editor, Tim Parker, publisher, and the rest of the efficient staff at Motorbooks International Publishing Office.

Foreword

They called it the *missile with a man in it*, and I had the privilege of being the first pilot to fly it.

I was chief engineering test pilot for Kelly Johnson's famed Skunk Works at Lockheed and had the opportunity to fly his aircraft on their first flights. Observing everything about a new airplane to determine the good and the bad factors that could affect its future—whether it was a topnotch design or an also-ran—was part of my job as a senior test pilot.

In late 1951, I was testing one of Lockheed's latest fighter planes at the aircraft test facility now known as the Air Force Flight Test Center at Edwards Air Force Base located next to the vast Rogers Dry Lake in California's Mojave Desert. The plane was the new F-94C Starfire, an interim all-weather fighter for the US Air Force Continental Air Defense Command. The Starfire had a limited life, however, because more advanced all-weather fighters were on the drawing board.

Lockheed had been building and testing jet-powered fighter planes for almost ten years, longer than any other US aircraft manufacturer. But Lockheed had not developed a successful new fighter since the XP-80 Shooting Star back in 1943. Kelly's staff of engineers wanted to rejuvenate their talents by creating a new and advanced fighter.

One day, during the Starfire tests, I ran into Kelly, my boss, in the middle of the ramp between our flight test hangar and the flight line at North Base. I told him what his engineers had told me. To support them, I voiced my own opinion. Kelly thought for a moment and said, "Tony, we are going to design a new

fighter. I don't know what it will look like, but we will build it—count on it!"

At the time, the United States and several other members of the United Nations were involved in the war with North Korea. Kelly had just returned from South Korea where he had studied the situation following the sudden appearance of the MiG-15, a Soviet jet-powered fighter flown by North Korea's air force.

American fighter pilots had complained to Kelly that the new MiG-15 could climb faster and fly higher than their fighter aircraft and was very maneuverable at high altitudes. The American pilots wanted Kelly to design and build a fighter that would outperform anything in existence.

In late 1952, Kelly called me and told me to pack my bag. "We are going up to Moffet Field [a naval air station near San Jose, California] to conduct some tests on a new type of in-flight aerodynamic simulator, and I want you to do those tests," he said. Kelly and his very capable aerodynamicist, Dick Heppe, in an effort to obtain complete objectivity in my flying analysis, wouldn't tell me what kind of airplane design I would be testing in this new computerized research aircraft.

The in-flight tests were a great success. Afterward, they told me the details they had been withholding.

The tests focused on a vastly new and revolutionary type of air superiority fighter that would dominate the skies for years to come. When Kelly and Dick showed me what it looked like, I could hardly contain my emotions. It had a long, streamlined, functional fuselage and a new type of empennage with the horizontal stabilizer mounted atop its

vertical tail called a *T-tail*. Its wing was hardly noticeable, it was so small in area and thin. Never before in the history of aircraft design had such an advanced concept of a fighter plane been considered except for some experimental research aircraft, with rocket propulsion, that had to be carried aloft by a mother plane for launch. The distinctive element of this new fighter design was the wing's dihedral—ten degrees downward.

When I asked Kelly about its strange wing, he responded, "Tony, that's why we're up here. You just became the first test pilot to contribute to the design of a jet fighter by use of the in-flight aerodynamic simulator you just flew." I was impressed with what I had just accomplished as well as eager for the day I would flight-test this new and exciting fighter plane that looked like it was doing Mach 2 just sitting still. The Air Force designated this sleek, missile-like airplane the F-104 and Lockheed named it Starfighter.

I watched the prototype XF-104 being built almost on a daily basis. Kelly wanted me to become as knowledgeable as possible with its various systems, many of which were new to fighter aircraft. Before I knew it, 27 February 1954 had rolled around—the date set for initial taxi trials. During a high-speed taxi the next day, the XF-104 made an unscheduled hop and flew about five feet off the ground for some distance. Its official first flight, however, didn't take place until five days later.

The first flight on 5 March 1954 went off with a few minor glitches, one of which was that the landing gear wouldn't retract. A second flight was made after some landing gear readjustments, but to

Whether you are a buff or a historian of military aviation, this historical chronicle of the *missile with a man in it* by Steve Pace is a must. With all best wishes for good reading about a fine fighter plane that was loved by the pilots who flew it.

Tony LeVier

Lockheed Aircraft Corporation hired Anthony William (Tony) LeVier in 1941 to ferry Royal Air Force Hudson bombers to Montreal, Canada. LeVier, who began his flying career in 1928 at the age of fifteen, became an engineering test pilot in 1942 and conducted extensive development flight tests on the P-38 Lightning—specifically, Allison engine development and dive tests to solve the compressibility problem.

LeVier later made the first flight on the XP-80A, as well as its subsequent Phase I development tests. He was promoted to chief engineering test pilot in 1945. He made the first flight on the Lockheed Saturn in 1946; the first flight as copilot on the Lockheed Constitution in 1946; the first flight on the Lockheed TF-80C (T-33A later) in 1948; and supervised the test pilot programs on all versions of the P-38 Lightning, F-80 Shooting Star, Constitution, Saturn, Constellation, and P2V (later P-2) Neptune.

LeVier then made the first flight on the XF-90 in 1949; the first flights on the F-94A and F-94B in 1948 and 1949, respectively; the first flight on the F-94C in 1951; the XF-104 Starfighter in 1954; the T2V-1 in 1954; and the U-2 in 1955.

LeVier became director of flying operations at Lockheed-California on 23 May 1955 and served in that capacity until 29 April 1974 when he retired after thirty-three years of faithful duty.

Tony LeVier has in excess of 10,000 flying hours and more than 24,000 flights in 260 different aircraft. He is a member of the Aviation Hall of Fame, and he is the president of S.A.F.E., Incorporated (Safe Action in Flight Emergency). He holds many awards and aviation-related memberships. Finally, LeVier is a pilot's pilot. I thank him for his participation in the preparation of this reference on the F-104 Starfighter.

Steve Pace

Tony LeVier poses with XF-104 number one circa 1955, following attachment of wingtip fuel tanks. LeVier explains, "The original XF-104 was a remarkable little plane. It was the first jet-powered plane to exceed 1,000mph [Mach 1.5], and I did it. I had misgivings about the plane at first, but after I got acquainted with it, it was super! We had lots of development problems as one might

expect, especially with the General Electric J79 series turbojet engines. Once everything was corrected, however, the plane was very well accepted by its pilots. And it's still being used today in several allied countries." LeVier left the Starfighter test program in early 1955 to concentrate on his next assignment—chief engineering test pilot on the Lockheed U-2 test program. Lockheed

no avail. The glitch sent the plane back to the drawing board for a brief time, which is normal for most new planes. With all of its systems finally in top shape, serious testing followed. The F-104 rewrote aviation history on almost every flight. I made the first flight exceeding 1,000mph, and eventually, the F-104 broke every world record for speed, altitude, and time-to-climb. It was, and still is, a fantastic machine, and I am thrilled to have been a part of its development.

Initially Kelly wanted me to flight-test his new aircraft because of the interest I took in the design of components that would be important to the operational pilots who would fly the fighters. For example, I invented an advanced warning system for aircraft and presented it to Kelly. He studied the design and wrote back, "It's the best design of a warning system I've ever seen; it'll go on the next airplane we build." I was pleased with his response, and sure enough, Kelly lived up to his word.

My Master Caution Warning Light System on the F-104 made it one of the

easiest fighter aircraft for a new pilot to check out in and fly correctly and to avoid the ever-present tendency to forget vitally important flight safety points.

The F-104 Starfighter was ordered in quantity to equip both the US Air Force Continental Air Defense and Tactical Air Commands. North Atlantic Treaty Organization (NATO) countries expressed great interest in the F-104, and the US government supplied many nations with Starfighters through the Military Assistance Program (MAP). Germany, Belgium, Italy, and the Netherlands built them in Europe under license. Canada and Japan did the same in their countries. This extensive interest in the F-104 set an ambitious manufacturing program into motion. Lockheed showed all licensed countries how to build the F-104s and furnished master tooling so parts made in one country would fit F-104s made in another. Eventually, fourteen foreign nations flew the Starfighter. Some of these countries still operate them.

Introduction

The Lockheed F-104 Starfighter was conceived as a dedicated air superiority fighter. As often happens, however, it was modified to perform a number of additional roles during its service life. These included fighter-interceptor, fighter-bomber, fighter-trainer, photographic reconnaissance, and the multi-mission, all-weather roles.

The advent of the experimental F-104 in 1954 reopened the controversy of the lightweight fighter concept. The question was whether the lightweight, small, sparsely equipped fighter was the answer to aerial combat tactics. The dispute had been born in the air battles fought over Korea. The Russian-built MiG-15 had outperformed the American-built F-86 Sabre because it was about two tons lighter than the Sabre and had a more powerful engine. In spite of this, Sabres ended the war with a seven to one kill ratio against the MiGs.

For some time, Lockheed had recognized that US Air Force (USAF) fighter aircraft were becoming too complex as well as too heavy. So Lockheed recommended a return to lighter fighter aircraft, stripped down but sufficiently armed, that could operate from forward air bases. These small fighters, if designed, would necessarily have the capabilities in their rates of climb, speeds, and service ceilings to outclass enemy fighters.

Without outside funding, Lockheed went to work in early 1952 to design a small fighter to fill this need. Whether the design would prove successful and whether the USAF would establish a requirement for it was questionable at best.

The answers to these questions came late in 1952 when the USAF, after looking at what Lockheed had proposed, did establish a requirement for a high-performance air superiority day fighter. Following a competition between Lockheed and its rivals, the Air Force ordered two experimental F-104s in early 1953. The need for such a fighter had been largely generated by the appearance of the MiG-15, which, although it lacked some of the complex equipment of the F-86, was a threat because of its outstanding performance.

To attain the desired performance, Lockheed designed the F-104 to use the General Electric J79 turbojet engine, an advanced afterburning powerplant. But since the J79 would not be available when the XF-104s were ready for flight-testing, Lockheed designed its two XF-104s around an interim powerplant, the afterburning Wright J65. But, the afterburning J65 would not be ready either; therefore, a transitory nonafterburning version of the J65 had to be employed so Lockheed could meet its contractual first flight commitment. And, in February 1954, XF-104 number one made an unofficial first flight of low altitude and short distance. Fortunately, the official first flight of XF-104 number one occurred shortly thereafter. The world at large, however, was not told of the occasion since the plane—and the event—was classified.

When an airframe contractor gets the opportunity to unveil a new and exciting airplane to the world, it customarily does so with a high-visibility roll-out party. But if the new airplane is classified, as often happens with Lockheed products, the general public knows nothing about it until the Department of Defense wants it to know. So Lockheed's prototype XF-104—a classified fighter airplane that would advance the so-called state of the art, smash all existing time-to-climb, altitude, and speed records, and render obsolete all existing fighter types with its matchless high-performance characteristics—remained a secret.

In 1956, the Department of Defense and the US Air Force finally lifted the veil of secrecy from its new and advanced, even radical, air superiority day fighter, and announced to the world the existence of the Lockheed F-104.

The F-104 was an instant hit with fighter pilots and quickly established Lockheed as a world leader in the design and development of advanced aircraft. The Starfighter was hot, a trendsetter, and its pilots respected it. When it first came into being, however, as with any new and advanced type of aircraft, the F-104 suffered from developmental problems such as powerplant malfunctions, armament problems, and high-speed and high-altitude instability; its original downward-firing emergency ejection seat system was its most unpopular feature. Design modifications overcame the F-104's problems for the most part. As a result, the F-104 went on to become the star fighter its namesake boasted.

This is the story of the Lockheed F-104 Starfighter.

Chapter 1

The XF-104: Birth of the Starfighter

Just before sunrise on the morning of 25 June 1950, North Korea, backed with military arms provided by the Soviet Union, attacked South Korea. Two days later, President Harry S. Truman ordered Gen. Douglas O. MacArthur to employ US land, sea, and air forces to help South Korea repel North Korea. To begin, MacArthur directed the USAF Far East Air Force (FEAF) to mount a series of air strikes with everything it had and to concentrate on North Korea's ground forces. This action began US involvement in the Korean War.

Clarence L. (Kelly) Johnson won the prestigious Robert J. Collier Trophy for the design of the Lockheed F-104 Starfighter in 1958. He won the Collier Trophy again five years later for the design of the A-12/YF-12/ SR-71 Blackbird series of aircraft. Lockheed

Five months later, six swept-winged jet-powered fighters identified as MiG-15s attacked a flight of World War II-era North American F-51 Mustangs just south of the Yalu River. The appearance of the MiG-15 came much sooner than anticipated. Worse, available FEAF fighter aircraft proved all but useless against them. Essentially, they said, the MiG-15 would gain and maintain local air superiority in short order if swept-winged jet-powered North American F-86 Sabres were not deployed to Korea at once.

Meanwhile, news of the early debut of the MiG-15 and its superiority over American fighters—mainly, the Lockheed F-80 Shooting Star and Republic F-84 Thunderjet—had filtered into the front offices of US aircraft manufacturers. For the most part, except for the F-86, all US fighters were instantly obsolete.

Clarence L. Johnson, founder and leader of the Advanced Development Projects (ADP) organization within Lockheed Aircraft Corporation, now Lockheed Advanced Development Company (LADC), more commonly known as the Skunk Works, had designed Lockheed's F-80.

On 8 November 1950, during the first jet-to-jet air battle in aviation history, an outclassed Lockheed F-80C Shooting Star that was piloted by USAF Lt. Russell J. Brown shot down a MiG-15 to record the first enemy jet kill of the Korean War. In this particular case, pilot skill had prevailed.

Understandably, Johnson was ecstatic when he learned that his creation had recorded the world's first jet-to-jet combat victory. However, with the arrival of the MiG-15, he knew his World War II-era design was now inferior.

He also knew the F-86 would have a rough go of it in Korea. And what about the future?

Johnson, who had been nicknamed Kelly by his friends in high school because he always wore green, asked for and received permission from Lockheed management to visit South Korea. He wanted to learn firsthand what FEAF fighter pilots actually wanted and needed in a fighter. He arrived in South Korea in November 1951, and to his surprise, found that they had already formed definite opinions. To a man, FEAF fighter pilots were wanting and needing a high-performance fighter that would trade weight and complexity for unmatched speed, altitude, and maneuverability. Lockheed, as it happened, had been thinking about such a fighter since early 1950. But the USAF had no requirement for a lightweight fighter—officially or unofficially.

Kelly Johnson returned home to Lockheed in December 1951 to discuss with management the fighter FEAF pilots had mentioned. He suggested that his firm design and propose to the USAF a new type of fighter plane so advanced in performance that it could not be ignored: an uncomplicated, lightweight, and inexpensive fighter that could outperform any projected fighter in the world. In essence, a star fighter. Johnson was authorized to proceed.

Johnson formed a team of first-rate Skunk Works engineers to initiate the program. In part, the team included Ed Baldwin, Dick Boehme, Phil Coleman, Henry Combs, Russ Daniell, Gene Frost, Willis Hawkins, Dick Heppe, Ben Rich, John Stroud, and Art Vierick. Bill Ralston was appointed as project engineer. These engineers were up for the task.

Starfighter Engines

Since an airplane can only be as good as its powerplant, the first order of business was to find a suitable turbojet engine for the fighter's propulsion system. Even though no fitting turbojet existed, several upcoming turbojet engines—all unproven—were under development for future applications. At first, with existing turbojet engines, Johnson's team set their goal on a fighter plane that could attain a maximum level flight speed of Mach 1.5, or one and one-half times the speed of sound. However, two forthcoming turbojet engines—the Pratt & Whitney J75 and the General Electric J79—were Mach 2 rated. Since level flight doublesonic speed was now a possibility for its proposed fighter, Lockheed investigated these two advanced turbojets for final application.

Since it was being promised sooner and met requirements, the General Electric J79 was selected. An outgrowth of the J73, known only as the J73-GE-X24A at the time, the proposed J79 was projected to produce at least 9,000lb military thrust and as much as 15,000lb afterburning thrust. It was the best engine of its day, and Lockheed's fighter would be designed to use it.

Airframe Design

Chief engineer Johnson and his stealthy engineering staff strived to design a provocative offering for USAF development. Thousands of configuration studies, wind tunnel tests, and flight simulations were engineered during 1952, with the emphasis placed on flexibility, growth potential, and safety. Lockheed knew from past experience with its P-38 Lightning and F-80 Shooting Star fighters that the key to success was to design a fighter with maximum kill probability for each taxpayer dollar invested. In addition to matchless performance, the new fighter needed range and armament equal to the next generation of supersonic jet fighters—the so-called USAF Century Series with designation numbers of 100 and above. If all went well, the new Lockheed fighter would receive one of these designation numbers.

After going through dozens of configurations, Johnson and his aerodynamicists first settled on

Richard T. Whitcomb, developer of the National Aeronautics and Space Administration (NASA) Area Rule theory, is shown with an F-104 wind tunnel model in the NASA-Langley wind tunnel. Though not mentioned in other references on the Starfighter, the F-104 used Whitcomb's "rule of thumb" to improve its performance in the transonic speed regime—600 to 800mph— where the airflow around an aircraft is most turbulent. NASA

Temporary Design Number (TDN) L-224. But this pre-predesign was shelved in favor of TDN L-227, which in turn became the predesign when they decided that TDN L-246 was best. What was to become the F-104 had been conceived.

Johnson's Skunk Works froze the TDN L-246 design on 30 October 1952. Lockheed's TDN L-246 was not only ahead of its time, it was ahead of its propulsion system—the J79 would not be available for several years—which meant an interim turbojet engine had to be found, which dictated the design of two different fuselage mid- and aft-sections, two different engine air intake and ducting systems, and two different engine exhaust pipe and outlet systems. One design was for the interim turbojet engine so its fighter could fly as soon as possible. The other was for the J79 engine when it became available.

Since the soon-to-materialize Wright Aeronautical J65-W-7 turbojet was being advertised to produce 10,300lb afterburning thrust (7,800lb military thrust), it was selected as the temporary propulsion system.

TDN L-246 Design Features

It took many configuration studies to lead Lockheed to TDN L-246 and its unique design features. Where TDN L-224 (the pre-predesign) was to have thirty-five-degree sweptback wings and tail surfaces, TDN L-227 (the predesign)

The Northrop Model N-102 Fang proposal was the F-104's strongest competition for the Weapon System 303A (WS-303A) contract. Like the Starfighter, it was to be powered by a General Electric J79 turbojet engine and armed with a General Electric M61 20mm Vulcan cannon. Its ventral, bifurcated engine air inlet is noteworthy. Northrop

featured sixty-degree delta wings and twin, outward-canted V-tails.

However, even in its interim frozen state, the Wright J65-powered TDN L-246 design bordered on the radical. With an empty weight of just 11,500lb, Lockheed's TDN L-246 design was a lean fighter. Lockheed eliminated every ounce of extra weight from its structure. In fact, it weighed half of the new breed of supersonic fighters' weight. And performance projections showed that it could climb at the same speed it could fly straight and level using military thrust alone—that is, Mach 0.90, without afterburning. Moreover, its design features and systems were revolutionary. Especially for the era.

It featured a very thin, trapezoidal wing with a thickness to chord ratio of only 3.36 percent, a quarter-chord sweepback of just eighteen degrees six minutes, no incidence, a leading-edge nose radius of only 0.016in and a razor-sharp trailing edge. And never seen before, a ten-degree negative dihedral (downward angle). The reason Lockheed opted for a negative dihedral wing was to improve roll control during high-g maneuvers in air-to-air combat; and, to augment stability at high speeds and high altitudes.

It also sported a T-tail arrangement whereby the tailplane mounted atop the vertical fin, just below the fin tip. And like the wing, the stabilator (combined stabilizer and elevator) was trapezoidal in planform. Lockheed selected this type of tail group to get the powered, all-moving horizontal tailplane into undisturbed airflow where wing-generated turbulence would not affect the fighters' lateral stability.

Its rocket-like fuselage was of a high fineness ratio—that is, highly tapered toward the nose to reduce frontal area as much as possible. Moreover, since the wings span much less distance tip-to-tip than the fuselage measures front-to-back, the wing aspect ratio is very low.

It was the first warplane to employ the six-barrel 20mm General Electric M61 (formerly T-171) Gatling-type Vulcan

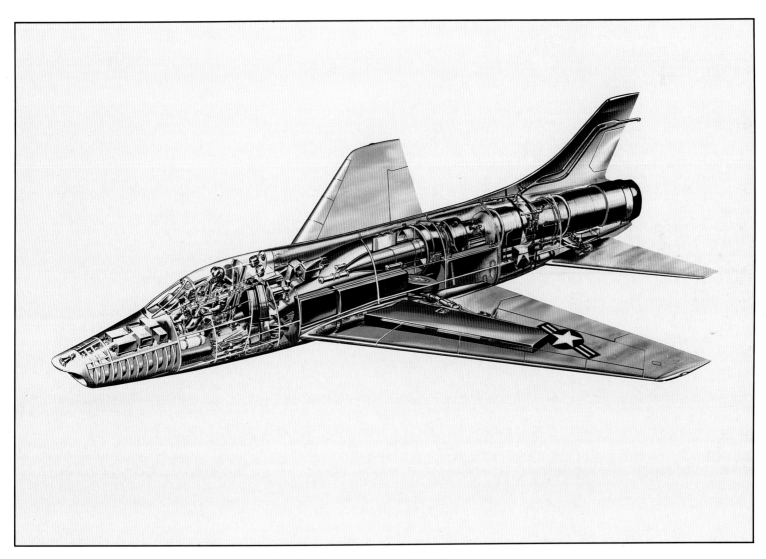

The North American Model NA-212 Super Sabre proposal was another finalist in the WS-303A competition. However, it too was passed over in favor of Lockheed's entry.

Notably, this version of the F-100 Super Sabre was modified to become the F-107 Ultra Sabre, which looked quite different. Rockwell

The Republic Model AP-55 was originally based on its Model AP-31 or XF-91 Thunderceptor (shown) but was soon replaced by a design that appeared in October 1953. For the WS-303A competition, *the final Model AP-55 featured a solid, rounded nose and NASA-developed flush-type engine air inlets, but otherwise, closely resembled the XF-91. USAF*

cannon, capable of firing up to 6,000 rounds per minute.

It was the first aircraft to use the General Electric J79 afterburning turbojet engine, initially capable of producing 9,300lb military thrust and 14,800lb afterburning thrust.

It was the first military aircraft to incorporate a downward-firing ejection seat system, later replaced by upward-firing ejection seat systems for pilot safety. Though unique at the time, and thought to be safe, the downward-firing ejection seat system proved to be unsafe, and deadly.

It was the first operational fighter, operational aircraft-period, capable of doublesonic (Mach 2) speeds. And it was the first operational fighter to sport jettisonable wing tip-mounted fuel tanks, and still fly supersonically. It was the first

fighter to employ wing tip-mounted missiles, and the first fighter to use boundary layer control to increase lift and decrease landing speed.

Finally, it was the first fighter to incorporate half-cones in engine air inlet to reduce the speed of the air entering the engine. These half-cones reduced Mach 2 airflow to about Mach 0.7 at the engine's face (YF-104A and on; not on XF-104s).

At the time, Ben Rich was a thermodynamic and propulsion engineer. (Ben Rich became Chief Skunk after Kelly Johnson retired in 1975. Rich retired in 1991, and at this writing, Sherm Mullin is Chief Skunk.) Rich and John Stroud designed the engine air inlets, ducts, and exhaust nozzle outlets for both the interim J65-powered and the design J79-powered versions of the fighter. The

unique T-tail configuration was designed by Kelly Johnson, Dick Heppe, Jim Hong, and Phil Coleman. Johnson, Heppe, and Coleman designed the wing's ten-degree negative dihedral. The high fineness ratio fuselage was designed by Johnson. According to Rich, and contrary to reports found elsewhere, the Douglas X-3 Stiletto research aircraft did not influence the TDN L-246 design. Skunk Works aerodynamicists did obtain some data from the Lockheed X-7 research missile, a test bed for various ramjet engines, which had only been flying for a short period at the time.

On 31 October 1952, Johnson presented TDN L-246 to Lockheed management for its scrutiny. He proudly presented a relatively simple airplane, optimized for the air superiority day fighter role. He knew the design was a good one and felt it could generate the long-term financial rewards his firm was needing. The trick was to get Lockheed management to approve the design so it could be presented to the USAF as an unsolicited proposal. Johnson went home that Friday night, handed out candy, and proceeded to enjoy his weekend.

Not knowing that Lockheed management had studied TDN L-246 over the weekend, Johnson returned to work on Monday with other things on his mind. Soon after his arrival, however, he was told that the design had already been approved. He was also told that he had been authorized to travel to Wright-Patterson Air Force Base (AFB) at Dayton, Ohio, to present Lockheed's unsolicited fighter proposal. Although Lockheed management was well aware that no requirement for such a fighter existed at the time, it strongly felt their offering was promising enough to create some real interest with the USAF Air Research and Development Command.

Selling the Starfighter to the Air Force

The USAF was truly swamped with new aircraft programs in November 1952—especially new fighter programs. These included the North American F-100 Super Sabre, a day fighter-interceptor; the McDonnell F-101 Voodoo, a long-range strategic fighter; the Convair F-102 Delta Dagger, an all-weather interceptor; and the Republic F-103, an all-weather interceptor. Moreover, it was dealing with North American, Republic, and Lockheed on the procurement and production of interim fighters from older designs to soldier on until the aforementioned fighter planes arrived—respectively, the F-86D Sabre, the F-84F Thunderstreak, and the F-94C Starfire. It would be a hard sell at best.

If you have ever tried to sell people something they did not need or know they wanted, then you know what Johnson was up against when he arrived at Wright-Patterson AFB on 5 November 1952. But he knew his firm had a good, even exceptional, design to offer. And being the good salesman he was, he commanded attention with his confident and straightforward sales pitch.

To begin, Johnson pointed out the current trend in fighter development practice, how forthcoming fighters were too complex, too large, too heavy, and too

The first F-104 Starfighter as it appeared shortly after its arrival at the restricted North Base Area of Edwards AFB. Its to-port-opening cockpit canopy is noteworthy, as is the original landing gear configuration. Lockheed

costly. Not forgetting the FEAF pilots he had talked with a year earlier, Johnson laid his firm's TDN L-246 proposal on the table and said, "Gentlemen, this is the type of fighter our boys are demanding." In part then, this is what Johnson offered.

• A small and light fighter airplane that would be relatively uncomplicated and inexpensive

• A high-performance fighter airplane optimized for the air superiority VFR (visual flight rules), or day, role. A fighter that could double as a day fighter-interceptor and a day photographic reconnaissance aircraft

• A single-seat, single-engine fighter pilot's fighter with unprecedented performance; able to outclimb, outrun, and fly higher than all other fighter aircraft with exceptional agility and maneuverability—a dogfighter in the truest sense of that phrase

Lockheed's proposal was well received. But, in order to obtain the fighter, the USAF had to devise a general operational requirement that called for a new tactical fighter to supplement and ultimately replace the USAF Tactical Air Command (TAC) F-100 Super Sabre (an aircraft that had not flown yet), beginning

in 1956. And, to be fair, it would have to invite bids from Lockheed's competitors.

In January 1953, Lockheed was notified by letter that its fighter proposal had been selected over all of the challengers' entries. Lockheed's proposal was just too seductive to pass up, and Lockheed's head start was just too great to overcome. In winning, Lockheed eliminated three strong entries from Northrop (Model N-102), North American (Model NA-212), and Republic (Model AP-55)—all finalists. The other entrants had been eliminated early.

Under Weapon System 303A (WS-303A), Lockheed was awarded letter contract AF-23362 for a full-scale engineering mock-up (already under construction with Lockheed funds), engineering data, wind tunnel and rocket-launched models, cockpit and armament mock-ups, one static loads test airframe, and two airworthy prototypes. At this time the experimental prototype fighters were designated XF-104. Lockheed designated the aircraft Model 083.

The XF-104

Actual construction on XF-104 number one began in the summer of 1953 at Lockheed's Burbank, California,

XF-104 Flight-Testing Begins

On 23 February 1954, following a classified communication to the Air Force Flight Test Center (AFFTC) headquarters at Edwards AFB, California, from the Lockheed Skunk Works that the number one XF-104 was ready for tests, Lockheed was authorized to secretly transport its experimental fighter to Edwards to begin Phase I and Phase III evaluations (see Table 1-1). Because the project remained classified, the Air Force directive specified that Lockheed carry out the activities at its own flight-test and evaluation facility at the restricted North Base Area within Edwards' vast boundaries. The secret directive also authorized Lockheed to transport the number two XF-104 to Edwards as soon as it was ready for testing; no red tape, just a telephone call to flight-test headquarters.

During the night of 24–25 February, Lockheed secretly trucked its number one XF-104 from Burbank to Edwards' North Base Area, where it was housed in a hangar for final assembly. While in the hangar, it was prepared for its low-, medium-, and high-speed taxi trials to check its nose-wheel steering, wheel brakes, and so on, prior to flight-test activity. At this time, it was powered by the nonafterburning Wright J65-B-3 turbojet engine being produced by the Buick division of the General Motors Corporation. The interim afterburning Wright J65-W-7 turbojet engine was not scheduled to arrive at Edwards until 1 June. The -7 engine was the USAF version of the Navy's J65-W-6 (the USAF uses odd suffix numbers and the Navy uses even suffix numbers). The -7 was to produce 7,800lb thrust without afterburning and 10,300lb thrust with afterburning; the afterburner section to the J65 engine was being developed by Wright Aeronautical, the powerplant division of the Curtiss-Wright Corporation.

Tony LeVier conducted the first low-speed taxi runs over Rogers Dry Lake on 27 February. In planned succession, LeVier completed seven low-speed taxi runs in increments of ten miles per hour between 40 and 100mph before the day was over. All went well and medium- to high-speed taxi runs were scheduled for the following day.

On 28 February, after a pair of runs to 110mph, LeVier took the XF-104 up to 120 and 125mph on the next two runs. A

XF-104 number two during an early test hop without its wingtip fuel tanks installed as yet. Its trapezoidal wing and stabilator planforms are shown to good advantage. This was the armament test bed, and on 14 April 1955, it was lost in a crash. Lockheed

facility; it was completed seven months later, on 23 February 1954. There were no construction problems.

Earlier, Lockheed appointed chief engineering test pilot Tony LeVier to be the XF-104 chief test pilot. LeVier, though eager to flight-test this new fighter, was understandably doubtful about its basic airworthiness because of the XF-104's radical design. But being a pilot's pilot, LeVier prepared himself to fly what was to become known as the *missile with a man in it*.

Kelly Johnson was even more concerned. Not because he was uncertain about his creation's ability to fly, but because he wanted to know if it would be a winner. He believed his firm had a world beater in the making, and he could not wait to see how hot it really was.

Lockheed's XF-104 design, the J65-powered Model 083-92-01, was unlike any fighter seen before. It featured a rocket-like fuselage, thin downward-angled wings, and an all-moving stabilator atop its vertical fin. It sported cheek-type

engine air inlets (one on either side of the fuselage), and a low-profile cockpit canopy.

Identical in appearance to air vehicle number one, construction on XF-104 number two—the armament test bed—began in the fall of 1953 but at a slower pace, in case revisions and additions to the basic design were necessary during its construction. XF-104 number two was completed in September 1954. XF-104 number two was built to evaluate the Vulcan 20mm cannon; number one was to evaluate the type's external wingtip-mounted fuel tanks (carriage, separation, and so on).

On 30 April 1953, during the final USAF mock-up inspection, Lockheed was instructed to substitute its planned armament of two 30mm cannons (one on either side of the fuselage) with a single T-171 (later M61) Vulcan 20mm cannon (on the left side of the fuselage)—projected to fire up to 6,000 rounds per minute—to be fed by a 725-round drum of ammunition.

third high-speed run, to 130mph, included a planned skip-off whereby XF-104 number one actually flew some five feet off the ground, straight down the lake bed for several hundred yards before LeVier returned it to terra firma. By contract, the XF-104 was to fly on this date, and it did.

After the taxi tests, the crew returned the airplane to its hangar to undergo static engine tests. The engine was removed from the airframe and installed in a stand for these test runs. A seat ejection test was also conducted before the airplane was cleared for its official first flight. This action was completed on the night of 4 March, and the first flight was scheduled for 0900 hours the following morning.

First Flight

On 5 March 1954, at 0900 sharp, LeVier rotated and took off in XF-104 number one. As had been planned, he was to retract the landing gear and evaluate the plane's basic flying characteristics. But the XF-104's landing gear refused to retract, and just twenty-one minutes later, he landed.

Lockheed technicians made landing gear adjustments, and the airplane was cleared for another test hop. LeVier took off again, and once more, the landing gear would not retract. So after some low-speed handling evaluations, he landed twenty-two minutes later and taxied the plane back to its hangar. LeVier also reported low fuel pressure.

The culprits were found to be a marginal fuel pressure regulator and low pressure in the hydraulic system. Both defects were corrected and the airplane was cleared for flight number three. However, inclement weather at Edwards grounded XF-104 number one until 26 March when flights three and four were successfully completed, with landing gear operating satisfactorily.

Early in April 1954, Bill Ralston, Lockheed's F-104 project engineer, reported flight-test activities during March 1954 as follows:

Tests were accomplished to determine the optimum yaw damper setting. The emergency landing gear extension system functioned satisfactorily on flights three and four but the emergency free-fall landing gear extension system failed to operate on flight four. The main landing gear actuating cylinders and the uplock were reworked as well as the nose landing gear uplock.

Difficulty was experienced with the fuel vent system and fuel tank pressurization system. Until rework can be accomplished, a wingtip ram vent has been incorporated. Engine operation has apparently been trouble free. Major problem areas appear to be with the landing gear retraction system, emergency free-fall landing gear extension system, fuel tank pressurization and venting system, and yaw damper operation.

LeVier conducted ten test flights on XF-104 number one during April 1954. Landing gear retraction and free-fall landing gear extension system tests proved unsatisfactory, but a subsequent design modification at Lockheed's Burbank facility corrected these problems. Corrective action on the number one XF-104 was made in the field; the same fixes on XF-104 number two were made during its construction.

During one of these flights XF-104 number one developed a fuel leak. To correct the problem on an interim basis, the two leaky twenty-five-gallon saddle tanks were removed from the fuselage, lowering XF-104 number one's fuel capacity to about 600 gallons. The XF-104's fuel leak problem was later cured and was not experienced by production aircraft.

The XF-104's original yaw damper was ineffective, allowing the nose to wander left and right. The problem was corrected with a revised rudder-centering device.

The braking parachute—deployed after touchdown to slow down the aircraft prior to braking—failed to deploy on flight fourteen. A 10ft-diameter parachute was initially used but proved inadequate. The 10ft chute was replaced with a 14ft-diameter braking parachute. It was this very same drag chute that failed to deploy on flight fourteen. The cause of that failure was believed to have been faulty parachute packing.

The highest indicated uncalibrated speed achieved through flight fourteen, still using the nonafterburning J65-B-3, was Mach 1.1 at 30,000ft during a descent. The maximum level flight speed reported was Mach 0.97 at 100 percent power (full military thrust) at 35,000ft. The longest flight was one hour and eighteen minutes on flight thirteen. The highest altitude reached was 42,000ft. After flight fourteen on 26 April 1954, flight-test activity on XF-104 number one was discontinued for installation of an

external tail cone fairing to further reduce boat-tail drag, an internal tail cone heat shroud, and the aforementioned rudder-centering device.

Seven test hops, flights fifteen through twenty-one, were flown during May 1954. On flight fifteen, the test pilot reported a definite improvement in yaw damper effect. But Lockheed was plagued with minor difficulties on XF-104 number one during these seven flights, which included a failure of the AN/ARC-34 radio. A lack of spare parts caused three test flights to be aborted, and several other flights to be canceled outright. Hydraulic pump leaks were recurring and caused cancellation of several scheduled test hops. A fourteen-foot-diameter drag chute with twenty percent porosity was installed after the chute failure on flight fourteen. No more chute-opening failures occurred, but the drag chute tended to oscillate after opening.

XF-104 number one's slow-flight characteristics were investigated to determine control response at low speeds. Observed results revealed a stall speed of 240mph at 25,000ft with about 3,400lb fuel onboard in the clean configuration (landing gear retracted and flaps at zero degrees). With landing gear and flaps extended, stall speed was reduced to 187.5mph at 16,000ft with 1,200lb fuel onboard. At 14,000ft with landing gear and flaps extended, the test pilot noted a stall speed of 180mph with 1,200lb fuel onboard. Stall warning buffet was experienced at these speeds with heavy buffeting at the lowest speeds—landing gear and flaps extended. However, the pilot reported that control response was positive at all test speeds.

Some vibration was noted when the speed brakes (one on either side of the aft fuselage) were fully extended. Data were obtained, however, to determine the correct speed brake opening deflection angle versus the amount of roughness.

Speed power points were made at 35,000ft at engine power settings between eighty-eight and 100 percent obtaining uncalibrated speeds from Mach 0.86 to 0.97. The highest reported speed prior to 31 May 1954 was Mach 1.2, obtained during a slight descent. Supersonic speed was easily attained during slight descents and the transition to supersonic speed was so smooth that the pilot might not notice it were it not for the Mach meter on the instrument panel. In other words, the airplane experienced no buffet while transitioning from subsonic to supersonic speeds.

Four test flights, twenty-two through twenty-five, were completed on XF-104 number one in June 1954. These test hops were all completed during the first ten days of the month. The balance of the month was used for installing engineering design changes dictated by the results of those four test flights.

The first takeoff and landing on a concrete runway came about on 2 June, providing photogrid data on takeoff and landing distances. Neither was made under maximum-performance conditions. Nevertheless, the data gave an indication of the aircraft's capability. Takeoff distance was 4,540ft with a full fuel load; landing distance was 2,515ft with 100 gallons of fuel onboard; corrected takeoff distance to clear a 50ft-high obstacle was 6,640ft. The afterburning J65-W-7 turbojet engine for XF-104 number one was still not available as of 30 June 1954.

The highest altitude attained for the airplane during June 1954 was 42,000ft. The fastest speed reported was Mach 1.26 in a descent from 42,000ft where the test pilot reported indicated air speed at Mach 1.1 passing through 40,000ft and registered 4.4g in a pull-out at 30,000ft at about Mach 1.1 during turns in both directions.

Also tested during June was the 16ft-diameter braking ribbon-type parachute originally used on the Lockheed F-94C Starfire. This parachute proved more effective than the 10ft and 14ft parachutes.

After flight twenty-five, on 10 June, XF-104 number one was grounded for further modification to the rudder-centering device, landing gear retraction system, ram air turbine (RAT) linkage, and hydraulic fluid system. A revised fuel control mechanism, new windshield panels, and new flight control system (FCS) control valves were also installed. An aileron roll damper and the afterburning J65-W-7 engine were expected to be installed when they became available.

In describing the number one XF-104 tested at Edwards through 30 June 1954, Kelly Johnson stated:

This is still a highly complex airplane. You simply do not fly around at 40,000ft at those kinds of speeds just by throwing a saddle over the thing and riding it. But what we have done is bring an end to the trend toward constantly bigger, constantly more complicated, constantly more expensive airplanes.

In July 1954, after the J65-B-3 turbojet engine had been replaced by the long-awaited afterburning J65-W-7 turbojet engine, Phase I and Phase III tests resumed. Just before grounding was lifted, the improved aileron roll dampers were installed along with a new pitch (nose-up, nose-down) limiter; the original yaw damper was retained.

During July 1954, a flight of 570 miles was conducted at a cruise speed of Mach 0.9 at 35,000ft to evaluate the aircraft's maximum range with internal fuel. During the month, the highest altitude attained was 52,000ft, and the highest level-flight speed was a true Mach 1.51 (1,000mph) at 40,000ft.

Phase II Flight-Testing

With the afterburning J65-W-7 turbojet engine installed, and a preproduction contract for seventeen service test YF-104As in hand, USAF Phase II testing began. Eight USAF evaluation flights were conducted in September and October 1954 to initiate Phase II.

Initial Phase II testing began on 24 September and was completed on 8 October, on XF-104 number one. These tests did not include an evaluation of the wingtip fuel tank installation because the tanks were not yet available. The results included a level-flight speed of Mach 1.49 at 41,000ft, and an altitude of 55,000ft was attained by zoom-climbing the airplane from 49,680ft with a climb speed of Mach 1.17.

After the first eight USAF Phase II tests were completed, the airplane was returned to Lockheed so it could conduct the wingtip fuel tank evaluations. Lockheed also investigated the aircraft's dynamic characteristics at high speeds without the yaw and roll dampers operating. Results prior to 31 December 1954 were not conclusive. Best speed of the number one XF-104 through 31

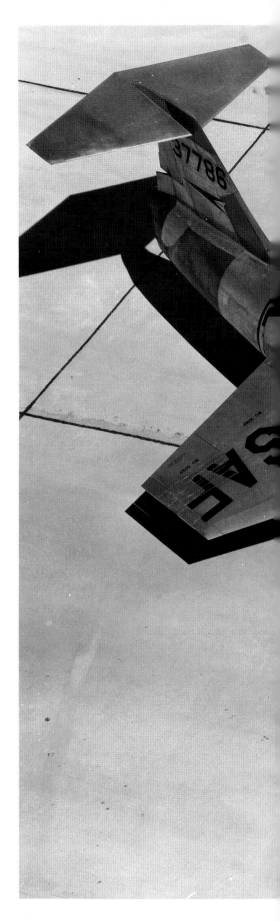

The engine air inlets for the Wright J65 turbojet engine show up well on the number one XF-104. This aircraft flew until 11 July 1957, when it was lost in a crash. This was the aerodynamic test bed. USAF via Marty Isham

December was reported to be Mach 1.6 in a dive.

Testing XF-104 Number Two

Earlier, on 4 October 1954, after the required telephone call to flight test headquarters, Lockheed received permission to move XF-104 number two to Edwards' North Base Area to begin testing. Tony LeVier piloted number two on its first flight two days later on 6 October. Number two had arrived complete with the afterburning Wright J65-W-7 engine and its maiden flight was successful.

As had been planned, XF-104 number two would be used to evaluate the new Vulcan 20mm cannon. Initial ground-firing tests were completed after successfully firing 2,500 rounds.

Aerial gun-firing tests were likewise satisfactory until flight four on 17 December. Three bursts had been fired at 30,000, 35,000, and 40,000ft altitudes. LeVier then climbed up to 43,000ft and pressed the trigger to fire a fourth burst. An explosion occurred, and the J65 engine began to run very rough so LeVier shut it down. Then after some seat-of-his-pants flying, gliding some fifty miles, LeVier made a successful dead-stick (unpowered) emergency landing on Rogers Dry Lake.

Post-flight investigation results showed that a single 20mm round had prematurely exploded and blew the cannon's bolt out the rear of the gun, through the aft bulkhead of the gun bay, and through the forward fuselage fuel cell. Jet fuel gushed into the gun bay, out the gun bay door joints, which had been sprung by the explosion, then into the left engine air inlet, flooding the engine with fuel and choking it to death.

In the meantime, Phase II testing on the number one XF-104 had proceeded. The Phase II tests were conducted in three segments. The first two segments were conducted in the clean configuration. The third portion was conducted with two 145-gallon wingtip fuel tanks installed; this was referred to as the tank configuration. Lockheed continued Phase I and Phase III tests on XF-104 number one when USAF Phase II tests were not being conducted. The three portions of the Phase II tests were flown as follows: 24 September to 8 October 1954, flights one through thirty; 15 to 19 February 1955, flights thirty-one

through thirty-five; and 15 to 18 March 1955, flights thirty-six through forty-one.

Upon the completion of Phase II testing, forty-one flights in just under six months, the XF-104 was evaluated as follows:

The capabilities of the XF-104 as a supersonic-class day air superiority fighter exceed those of any other known turbojet-powered aircraft.

The handling characteristics of the aircraft throughout the speed range with the yaw and roll dampers operating are very satisfactory. The preciseness, ease of operation, and general feel of the powered flight control system is notable.

The possibility of longitudinal [nose-left/tail-right, nose-right/tail-left] control problems exists. Care must be exercised in production quality control of the FCS components. The proper operation of yaw and roll dampers is essential to operation of the XF-104 as a tactical weapon.

Takeoff, recovery from all operational speeds, and landing with the dampers off can be safely accomplished, but the plane is not suitable for any tactical purposes in this configuration. The unpowered rudder does not furnish directional control at high indicated air speeds or Mach numbers [subsequent F-104 production aircraft employed powered rudders].

The capabilities of the XF-104 as a subsonic-class day air superiority fighter are exceeded by USAF fighters currently operational. The major deficiency of the XF-104 is the lack of thrust both at military and afterburning power to fully utilize the tactical capabilities of the XF-104's aerodynamic configuration.

The lack of thrust is manifested in the relatively low service ceiling, the small load factor attainable at high altitude without loss of energy [speed] or altitude, and the time required to accelerate to speeds above Mach 1.3.

The handling characteristics with the wingtip fuel tanks installed are acceptable within the limits tested. The present flight limitations render the tanks unsuitable for tactical usage. The aircraft should be placed in production as soon as an engine [the GE J79] is available with sufficient thrust to give supersonic combat capabilities without the use of afterburner.

Other significant conclusions reached in regard to the XF-104 fighter were as follows:
• The rate of climb, speeds attainable in level flight, speeds attainable at high altitude, maneuverability at supersonic speeds, and ability to retain speed during maneuvers at supersonic speeds were outstanding.
• Trim changes when encountered were mild and easily controlled.

• The utility of and visibility from the cockpit were satisfactory and equalled or exceeded production fighters.
• Subsonic maneuverability above 25,000ft was insufficient to allow the aircraft to adequately defend itself.
• The unpowered rudder did not furnish directional control at high air speeds or Mach numbers because of the forces involved. The rudder break-out forces were too high, and the feel of the locking action was detrimental to smooth control when small deflection movements were required.

On 15 March 1955, XF-104 number one established a program highlight. For on that date, XF-104 number one recorded the highest level-flight speed recorded by either XF-104 aircraft. Powered by the interim afterburning Wright J65-W-7 turbojet engine, the plane attained Mach 1.79 at 60,000ft. This feat was accomplished by Lockheed test pilot J. Ray Goudey.

That outstanding event in the XF-104 flight-test program was soon overshadowed, however, by the crash of number two on 14 April 1955. As it happened, Lockheed test pilot Herman R. (Fish) Salmon was performing a gun-firing test at 50,000ft. As he pressed the trigger, severe vibrations began because of a malfunction with the gun. Those vibrations were enough to shake loose the ejection hatch on the belly of the plane just below Salmon. Since he was at high altitude, and in a high-altitude pressure suit, his suit pumped up and over his face where he couldn't see. Remembering LeVier's experience earlier when a 20mm round had exploded prematurely, Salmon believed he had experienced the same fate. He didn't know his ejection seat hatch was gone, believing instead that part of the plane had blown off. His anticipation of the worst convinced him to eject. He did and parachuted to safety. XF-104 number two, though, was a total loss. After the event, Salmon found out that he could have saved the plane by simply lowering his altitude, waiting for his pressure suit to deflate, and safely land it.

Since XF-104 number one was not equipped with either the 20mm Vulcan cannon or the AN/ASG-14T-1 fire control system (it was loaded with test equipment instead), and because no service test YF-104As were yet available, a Lockheed F-94C was modified to serve as the F-104's armament test bed on an interim basis.

20

After some twenty-three months of classified XF-104 test flights and evaluations, the USAF scheduled a roll-out ceremony for 16 April 1956 at Lockheed's Burbank facility. The public would not see the last surviving XF-104, however. Instead, it would see the much sleeker YF-104A. In fact, as it came about, the public would not even see a photograph of an XF-104 until after its formal flight-test and evaluation program had ended on 31 August 1956.

Tragically, after accumulating nearly 1,000 flying hours, XF-104 number one was lost in a crash. At the time, the number one XF-104 had been experiencing vertical fin flutter at high speed and altitude. Because of this, its maximum speed had been limited to Mach 0.95 at no higher altitude than 20,000ft. On 11 July 1957, it was being used as a chase plane for ongoing F-104A flight-test activities. Piloted by Lockheed's William M. (Bill) Park, the

aircraft's vertical fin flutter condition set in during the chase flight, and the entire tail group fluttered off. Loss of control was immediate, and Park was forced to eject. Slightly injured, Park survived the ordeal to continue his flight-test activities for Lockheed's Skunk Works, flying some of its more interesting aircraft, including the *Have Blue* technology demonstrator prototype of the F-117A Stealth Fighter.

Because of its flutter condition, Tony LeVier had tried to remove number one

Both XF-104 prototypes during a Lockheed photo flight near Edwards AFB in early 1955. XF-104 number one has early style wingtip fuel tanks installed; XF-104 number two is *clean. At this time, both aircraft were powered by the afterburning Wright J65-W-7 turbojet engine. Lockheed*

from flight status—to place it in an aviation museum. Besides, he said, "Its flutter condition, coupled with its speed and altitude restrictions, made it unworthy of chase plane activities with faster and higher flying F-104A aircraft." But his argument went for naught. Thus, since both prototype XF-104s had been lost, at least one aviation museum lost out on having an original Starfighter for one of its most treasured displays. Nevertheless, the F-104 story does not end here.

Test Phases

Phase I—Air Worthiness: Flight test conducted by the contractor to determine the aircraft's ability to fly safely.

Phase II—Contractor Compliance: Flight tests whereby the US Air Force test pilots fly the aircraft to determine if it meets the performance guarantees.

Phase III—Design Refinement: Conducted by the contractor, using the same aircraft as in Phases I and II, to overcome deficiencies noted during the previous tests.

Phase IV—Performance and Stability: Flight test to obtain detailed data on the aircraft's performance and handling qualities.

Phase V—All-Weather: Tests to ascertain the aircraft's limitations under conditions of adverse weather.

Phase VI—Functional Development: Focuses on the tactically equipped production aircraft and identifies previously undiscovered shortcomings. Also included in this phase is the aircraft's durability, maintainability, logistical support, and so forth.

XF-104 Specifications

Crew	One
Wingspan	21.94ft (without wingtip fuel tanks)
Wing area	196.10sq-ft
Length	49.17ft
Height	13.49ft
Empty weight	11,500lb
Gross weight	16,700lb
Maximum speed	Mach 1.79 (attained)
Armament	One 20mm M61 Vulcan cannon (XF-104 number two)
Powerplant	One Buick-built Wright J65-B-3 (XF-104 number one only); one Wright J65-W-7 (both XF-104s after XF-104 number one was re-engined)
Number built	Two

Chapter 2

The YF/F-104A Starfighter

The Korean War ended on 27 July 1953, about eight months before the start of XF-104 flight-testing. So, for the most part, the immediate requirement for a high-performance air superiority fighter became null and void. And, because of this reality, Lockheed did an about-face—that is, it changed the basic mission of the F-104 from (1) air superiority to (2) air defense—just the reverse. In doing this, Lockheed now offered its F-104 as an air defense fighter-interceptor able to double as an air superiority fighter if required. It was an ingenious and logical sales method that worked because Lockheed knew the USAF needed an interim fighter-interceptor to fill the void between the Convair F-102 Delta Dagger and its replacement, the Convair F-106 Delta Dart.

Meanwhile, XF-104 flight-testing had proceeded steadily. Simultaneously, Lockheed was dealing with the USAF on a buy of seventeen service-test YF-104As, seven preproduction F-104As, and up to 698 production F-104As (by 1957, the programmed production run of all single-seat F-104As stood at 722; however, this total was later reduced to 170 because of budget cuts). On 30 March 1955, USAF contract AF-27378 was approved for seventeen single-seat service-test YF-104A aircraft; contact number AF-27378. One year later, on 2 March 1956, contract AF-30756 for seven preproduction F-104As was approved by the USAF. The contract also authorized the procurement of 146 F-104As, six tandem-seat F-104Bs, and fifty-six single-seat production F-104Cs (more on these two versions later).

It was late 1955 before General Electric began shipping its service test YJ79-GE-3 turbojet engines to Lockheed for installation in the YF-104As. The first YF-104A was completed in February 1956 and trucked to Edwards AFB for Phase I and Phase III contractor testing.

On 17 February 1956, after some twenty-three months of secret flight-test activities on the two prototype XF-104s, and two days after the crash of XF-104 number two, the first YF-104A made its maiden flight with Lockheed's Herman "Fish" Salmon under glass. It was a much different airplane.

YF-104A Rollout

One day earlier, on 16 February, the USAF finally lifted its two-year-long veil of secrecy off its new Starfighter in a media-covered rollout ceremony at Lockheed's Burbank plant.

When the F-104 appeared publicly for the first time, people were listening to

The number two YF-104A during its first flight. This was the first Starfighter seen by the general public as it was used for the official F-104 rollout ceremony in early 1956. Lockheed

23

a new sound called rock 'n' roll. It was the rockin' fifties, and when the Starfighter rolled out, it rocked those in attendance. Attending air enthusiasts were astounded by what they saw. At first glance, the aircraft did not look like it had wings, or like it would fly. Moreover it had covers faired over its engine air intakes on either side of the fuselage to hide its half-cones (these covers were immediately dubbed *flight falsies*, and today, remind us of rock singer Madonna's bullet-shaped brassieres). It featured downward-angled wings, a high T-tail, and its rocket-like fuselage was much longer than its wingspan. In truth, it looked more like a missile than an airplane: It looked like it was going Mach 2 just sitting static on the ramp.

Questions were immediately raised about the so-called flight falsies, but went unanswered. The USAF simply did not want the configuration of the F-104's engine air inlets, with their trick shock cones, made known at the time because it was a new and improved method of slowing down the air entering the ducts.

Since the public had not seen the XF-104 before the number one YF-104A was unveiled at Burbank, it did not realize that the aircraft had undergone many design changes before its debut. The fuselage had been lengthened 5ft, 6in to accommodate the J79 engine, its nose gear now retracted forward instead of aftward for improved ejection seat clearance out its bottom, two additional fuel cells were added in the fuselage, and

it sported new engine air inlet and exhaust outlet systems.

YF-104A Flight-Testing

Still skeptical about the Starfighter's service suitability because of its advanced design features, performance, and its new engine, the USAF demanded extensive developmental tests before the type would enter full-scale production and service. Although it had the potential of becoming the hottest fighter the world had ever known, it didn't dispel the USAF's need for caution. The USAF's action turned out to be a prudent one.

Eleven days after the first flight of YF-104A number one, on 28 February

The number one YF-104A on Rogers Dry Lake at Edwards AFB. Its faired-over 20mm cannon port and revised engine air inlets for J79 propulsion are noteworthy. USAF

1956, it exceeded Mach 2. Thus, the Starfighter became the world's first fighter airplane capable of doublesonic speed in level flight.

All seventeen YF-104A aircraft were used to flight-test and evaluate three early versions of the General Electric J79 turbojet (the -3, -3A, and -3B), the then-new 20mm Vulcan cannon, the relatively new AIM-9 (formerly GAR-8) Sidewinder air-to-air missiles and wingtip-mounted fuel tanks, and to explore the fighter's entire performance envelope.

During February 1956, contractor Phase I and Phase III activities were activated for the service test F-104As at Edwards AFB. On 24 April 1956, some two months after the first flight of the number one YF-104A, Flight Test Center

commander Brig. Gen. J. Stanley Holtoner advised Air Force Systems Command commander Lt. Gen. Thomas A. Power that there had been slippage in the flight-test program of the YF-104A because of compressor problems with the J79 engine. In a 15 June 1956 letter to Power, Holtoner wrote:

The F-104A has made eighteen flights to date for a total flying time of eleven hours and fifty-five minutes. Engine life has averaged approximately three flights. The maximum design speed of Mach 2.01 at 40,000ft was reached with these early low-thrust engines. The maximum altitude to date is 55,000ft. It was accomplished by flying at Mach 1.94 at 40,000ft, starting a climb and bleeding off airspeed. At 55,400ft, the machine was still going Mach 1.83. A single flight with the higher thrust

engine [-3B] had to be cut short on account of vibration. However, the pilot felt that climb and acceleration were improved. The contractor has not yet obtained any data on spins, pitch-up, or inertial coupling. We should begin our evaluation [Phase II] in July [1956].

In addition, Holtoner wrote:

One such climb was started at 58,000ft at Mach 2; the J79 afterburner blew out at 63,000ft but the climb was continued to an indicated 70,800ft [at 337.5mph indicated airspeed] before starting down. The highest indicated airspeed attained was 1,065mph during a level turn at 2.2gs at 30,000ft [Mach 1.9].

In conclusion, Holtoner wrote:

Maximum g imposed during these tests was 4.0g. External tanks were not available for the tests. With internal fuel only, limited endurance and radius of action pose

With its J79-GE-3 turbojet engine in afterburner, YF-104A number eleven does a nighttime engine run-up test at Edwards.

Hold-back cables were attached to its main landing gear struts to keep it from taking off. USAF

25

YF-104A number eleven during a test flight at Edwards AFB. Note ventral fin for improved directional stability. USAF

serious problems in any proposed tactical utilization of the aircraft. It appears that, with internal fuel only, the F-104 might have an intercept radius of 150 miles against a B-52 type target at 45,000ft. Intercepts at 70,000ft would have to be made over the base. Provisions for additional internal fuel and early development of satisfactory external tanks are a must for this aircraft. Another problem area which has not as yet been explored is that of pitch-up at high angles of attack.

Deficiencies of the YF-104A

A two-week flight evaluation of the automatic pitch control system in the YF-104A aircraft was started in early December 1956. Both the number one XF-104 and the number three YF-104A were used for the tests. Every possible attempt was made to achieve a condition where pitch-up occurred in spite of the warning (stick shake) and corrective action provided by the pitch control system. No effort was made to overpower the automatic pitch control system during the tests—that is, to override the system for manual control. Minimum maneuvering speeds and limited normal

accelerations at all speeds were measured as limited by the pitch control system.

From the above test program, it was possible to determine the effectiveness of the pitch control and also how much the system limited maneuverability. When that evaluation was completed, Lockheed agreed to proceed with the pitch-up and spin demonstrations.

The pitch-up demonstration called for the aircraft to be completely stalled by slowing it down to where a g break, roll-off, or pitch-up occurred for a series of conditions starting at 1.0g at 40,000ft and Mach 0.6 and working up to 1.0g at 60,000ft at Mach 0.95, then increasing g and Mach number in increments to 2.0gs at 60,000ft at Mach 1.4. Modifications to the plan were to be made as new information were obtained from each flight.

During an early Lockheed flight test on XF-104 number one, before the automatic pitch control system had been installed, Tony LeVier had the misfortune of experiencing a violent pitch-up. While flying a series of wind-up turns, or WUTs, he reached an altitude of about 50,000ft

and a speed of about Mach 0.95 when the pitch-up occurred without warning. He said, "The nose pitched up to a very high angle of attack in an instant. Then in about 1.5 seconds, the airplane snap-rolled twice. I was able to regain control, however, by pushing forward on the stick. I won't ever forget that maneuver."

Because steady spins had not resulted from pitch-up test maneuvers, separate flights were programmed with attempts to kick the aircraft into a spin before the stall had progressed into a pitch-up. Every effort was to be made to spin the aircraft so that possible recovery techniques would be known before the F-104A was placed in service.

In his letter to Lieutenant General Power, dated 7 December 1956, Brigadier General Holtoner emphasized the following:

Spectacular speed and climb performance have given many people a misleading impression of the present operational capabilities of the F-104A. In addition to the pitch-up problems to be solved before the aircraft are ready for service, delays in the development of wingtip tanks, pylon tanks [underwing], and adequate armament [cannon and wingtip-mounted missiles] will relegate early production aircraft to little more than a training role. Eight early production F-104As are to be delivered to us for testing in January and February [1957], six for Phase VI functional development tests and two for Phase IV performance and stability tests.

By 5 December 1956, twenty-four F-104A aircraft (seventeen YF-104As and seven F-104As) had been delivered for test activities. However, the Flight Test Center reported that "the first thirty-six aircraft [including twelve production F-104As] will not be capable of assuming tactical responsibility and the test inventory was increased to include these additional aircraft. Follow-up contracts for production articles are in effect."

The USAF Air Defense Command (ADC) was scheduled to receive operational F-104As before the USAF Tactical Air Command (TAC). The only proposed external change between ADC and TAC F-104As was provisions for Sidewinder missiles on the ADC aircraft.

Special Weapon Configuration

As of 5 December 1956, the Special Weapon Configuration had not been finalized and no proposed test program had been scheduled. The F-104A was designed to carry a single B28 (formerly T28) or B28-1 (formerly T28-1) nuclear bomb and/or wingtip and underwing auxiliary fuel tanks.

This program was designed to obtain performance and stability data representative of Tactical Air Command's single-seat F-104C (discussed in Chapter 4) with external stores, and to determine separation characteristics of the nuclear ordnance throughout the proposed operating envelope. Since no F-104C aircraft were available at the time, F-104A serial number 56-0801 was used for the performance phase and F-104A serial number 56-0790 was used for the stability phase; both aircraft were powered by the J79-GE-3A engine. Both aircraft were equipped with external ventral bomb racks to carry the B28. Additional fuel was carried externally in two 165-gallon wingtip tanks and two 200-gallon underwing pylon tanks; internal fuel was 908 gallons.

The B28 nuclear bomb, designed to be dropped from high-altitude at subsonic or supersonic speeds, was 170in long, 20in in diameter, and weighed 2,013lb. The B28-1, a parachute-drop bomb, designed to be delivered at low altitude under high-g conditions (using the low-altitude bomb system or LABS), was 175in long, 20in in diameter, and weighed 2,195lb.

The Special Weapon Configuration program required thirty-seven flights totaling thirty-seven hours and thirty minutes. It was conducted at Lockheed's Palmdale, California, facility and at Edwards AFB. Upon completion of the test program, test personnel evaluated the performance of the F-104A with the B28 and B28-1 stores and external fuel tanks as follows:

Performance of the F-104A with a special store and four tanks is greatly reduced as compared to the clean aircraft with the exception of the range available in a mission with 1,638 total gallons of internal/external fuel. The maximum [afterburning] power sea level rate of climb is reduced from 36,400 feet per minute (fpm) for the clean aircraft to 23,400fpm for the aircraft with five external stores.

The aircraft had no supersonic capabilities with the five external stores attached; however, limited supersonic speed [about Mach 1.2] is available with just the [nuclear] store and wingtip tanks installed. The maximum speed obtained with only the store installed was Mach 1.91. Supersonic performance is very costly in terms of fuel and time, and therefore range with the store installed.

By dropping the external fuel tanks as they become empty in a typical subsonic combat mission, the store may be dropped on a target 828 miles from the home base and the aircraft returned safely.

There are no serious stability and control problems throughout the normal subsonic and supersonic envelope with the store installed. However, the aircraft fishtails at speeds above 675mph IAS [indicated airspeed] when any of the external tanks are carried along with the store.

Maximum level flight speed using military power with the store was about Mach 0.965 at 20,000ft and Mach 0.945 at 35,000ft. Approximately 3.23 minutes and 1,090lb of fuel were required to accelerate from Mach 0.9 to Mach 1.7 at 35,000ft. The distance traveled was 60.75 miles.

Ongoing YF-104A and F-104A Developments

Earlier, the number one YF-104A (serial number 55-2955) was used for USAF Phase II contractor compliance evaluation. The flight-test program consisted of eighteen flight-test hours and ended on 21 August 1956. In the meantime, aircraft modifications included the installation of a ventral fin to improve directional stability at supersonic speeds and a number of flap-blowing boundary layer control systems to help overcome the type's small wing area and reduce the inherently high sink rate and landing touchdown speed.

In December 1956, Phase IV and Phase VI tests were set in motion at Edwards. For Phase IV, performance and stability tests were performed on YF-104A number eleven (serial number 55-2965) and YF-104A number twelve (serial number 55-2966). For Phase VI, functional development tests were performed on YF-104A number seventeen (serial number 55-2971), three *test* F-104As (AF 56-733/-734/-736), and two early production F-104As (AF 56-737 and 56-741). These aircraft, according to the Flight Test Center report, "will have operational armament and fire control systems installed. Each aircraft will be flown approximately 150 hours for a total of 900 hours for the program."

Even after all this testing and development, much more was necessary before the F-104A was ready for service. Also it was known that various aspects of flight generated high risk, and consequently, the Flight Test Center outlined its position as follows:

Flight evaluations will be performed on Phase III design refinement developmental aircraft assigned to the contractor to the extent and at such times as may become necessary to monitor properly the development of the Weapon System. These evaluations will be performed by the Flight Test Center at such places as may be designated. The aircraft and necessary instrumentation will be maintained by the contractor.

The following types of flight are considered as high-risk flights: (1) pitch-up, (2) spins, (3) structural demonstrations, (4) altitude flights above 50,000ft, (5) flight envelope expansions, (6) weapon firing, (7) stores jettisoned, and (8) dead engine landings. These eight types of flights should be chased by AFFTC aircraft; however, if chase aircraft are not available, Lockheed would be granted permission to use their own aircraft with a qualified pilot in order to expedite the program. On pilot checkouts, it is felt that Lockheed should furnish chase aircraft if possible and that an experienced Lockheed F-104 pilot would be the pilot of the chase plane[s].

YF-104A Disposition

As previously mentioned, seventeen service test YF-104A aircraft were produced. Of these, after their respective flight-test and evaluation programs, there are only two known survivors. The number seven YF-104A (serial number 55-2961) was used by the National Aeronautics & Space Administration (NASA) from August 1956 through November 1975. It now resides at the National Air and Space Museum, Washington, D.C. The number thirteen YF-104A (serial number 55-2967) is displayed at the Air Force Academy, Colorado Springs, Colorado.

At least four YF-104As (serial numbers 55-2956/-2957/-2969/-2971) were transformed into unmanned QF-104A target drones and were most likely shot down in air-to-air gun or missile firing tests. The number eleven YF-104A (AF 55-2965) went to the USAF Test Pilot School, and its fate is unknown.

Finally, after their respective evaluations, most YF-104As were brought up to production F-104A standards. In fact, according to official USAF documentation, no mention is made of YF-104As, only of F-104As. Yet, the seventeen service test aircraft were officially designated YF-104A when they were ordered. Likewise, most of the seven preproduction test F-104As were brought up to production F-104A standards. Those YFs and test F-104A aircraft that had been brought up to production F-104A standards were ultimately deployed to operational USAF squadrons.

Production F-104A

At a time when contemporary fighter aircraft were hard-pressed to attain supersonic speed in level flight, the Air Force appreciated the F-104A's outstanding performance. In fact, its speed during climbs was equal to its speed during straight-and-level flight. And, instead of struggling to achieve supersonic speed, it easily surpassed doublesonic speed; it could also maneuver and fight at such speeds.

Approved 2 March 1956, the USAF ordered 146 production F-104As. This brought the total F-104A procurement to 170 aircraft.

As F-104A production moved forward, General Electric developed a more reliable and higher thrust version of its J79. Known as the -3B, this version of the J79 was retrofit in production F-104As as they became available, beginning in April 1958. As it happened, the earlier -3 and -3A versions of the J79 were responsible for several crashes and in-flight emergencies during testing, even after the F-104A had met its initial operational capability. Flameouts, oil depletions, and ignition failures to these two versions of the J79 were a serious and constant problem.

YF-104A number one taking off from the main runway at Edwards. Ventral fin has not yet been added to this Starfighter; landing gear has just begun to retract. USAF

28

F-104A Armament

Although it had been optimized to serve as a daytime air superiority fighter, it was known all along that the F-104 could clearly be adapted for intercept, ground attack, or tactical support duties. It could carry a variety of armaments, including nuclear air-to-air missiles and free-falling nuclear bombs. Simply, the F-104A was to be a complete weapon system capable of carrying everything from conventional bombs to nuclear bombs, conventional missiles to nuclear missiles, and cameras to external fuel tanks.

General Electric, though able to solve its J79 engine woes, was not able to quickly cure the problems associated with its M61 Vulcan 20mm cannon. These problems were excessive vibration and premature detonation of 20mm ammunition during aerial gun-firing tests.

Primarily, these problems were attributed to the cannon's inability to handle high-g stresses during various combat maneuvers completed in its early developmental period. And since the cannon was too unreliable for service use in early production Starfighters, the USAF decided against their installation on 1 November 1957. In 1964, however, after the much improved and more reliable M61A1 had been developed and

YF-104A number seventeen on 1 October 1958 after its fourteenth barrier run test at Edwards AFB; Lockheed's Jim Wood was the pilot and survived this ordeal. Later, this YF-104A was converted into one of twenty-four QF-104A target drones. DoD via Robert F. Dorr

A production F-104A closes in on Republic YF-105A number two for an in-flight test of the fighter-to-fighter in-flight refueling system. This activity made feasible the F-104C's and F-104D's probe-and-drogue in-flight refueling capability. USAF

The Proposed RF-104A

On 6 December 1956, the Flight Test Center published its position on the proposed single-seat RF-104A photographic reconnaissance plane. But even at that time the RF-104A program was uncertain, though tentative schedules had indicated that a pair of service test YRF-104As would be built by

approved for service, the F-104's basic armament package became complete.

Lockheed in 1957, with production delayed until 1958.

At the time it was believed that the YRF-104As would have the Phase I engine (J79-GE-3A) and some of the production models would have the Phase II engine (J79-GE-3B). Since this was to be a high-speed reconnaissance aircraft, the viewfinder system in the service test examples would have been optical; however, later production models were to be equipped with a television-type viewfinder system.

The reconnaissance version of the Starfighter would have carried no armament. In creating the reconnaissance version of the F-104, the configuration change was to be forward of the aft end of the cockpit section only. Although the differences between the F-104A and the proposed RF-104A were to be minor, it was believed that a USAF Phase II contractor compliance test would have been required on the photographic reconnaissance model.

An F-104A on 21 January 1958 at Edwards AFB in preparation for tests of AIM-9

Sidewinder air-to-air missiles and M61 20mm Vulcan cannon. USAF via Marty Isham

Lockheed had initiated design work on its proposed RF-104A (Model 383-93-04) in November 1954. In January 1957, however, the contract for eighteen aircraft (AF 56-939 through 956) was canceled. That action occurred before the first service test YRF-104A had been completed. The RF-104A program was terminated in favor of the McDonnell RF-101 Voodoo—specifically the RF-101C, which carried much more reconnaissance equipment for much longer distances than Lockheed's proposed star gazer.

Improvements

Production F-104As featured a number of improvements over the seventeen YF-104As, and the seven preproduction F-104As. These included:
• Strengthened airframe, stressed for 7.33gs maneuvering
• Addition of an aft-mounted ventral fin on centerline to improve directional stability at high speed and high altitude
• Various flap-blowing boundary layer control systems
• Installation of the "interim" AN/ASG-14T-1 fire control system, later

replaced with the fully capable AN/ASG-14T-2 fire control system
• Incorporation of the J79-GE-3B turbojet engine, replacing the J79-GE-3 and J79-GE-3A turbojets

Later improvements included the aforementioned installation of the improved General Electric M61A1 20mm Vulcan cannon beginning in 1964 because the early M61 cannons proved unreliable and were either not installed or were removed as of 1 November 1957 before any single-seat F-104As were delivered to operational squadrons; and the replacement of the downward-firing ejection seat system with an upward-firing ejection seat system.

Before the single-seat F-104A Starfighter could enter service with the Air Defense Command as a daytime fighter-interceptor, more than 6,500 flight-test evaluations had to be performed, and more than two million engineer-hours had to be expended. By the time the F-104A entered USAF service in early 1958, it was a fully capable daytime interceptor armed with air-to-air missiles to defend America against an enemy nuclear bomber attack.

F-104A Enters Service

Two years late, beginning on 26 January 1958, the single-seat F-104A entered operational service—not with Tactical Air Command as originally planned (it had been scheduled to replace F-100s beginning in 1956), but with Air Defense Command. This change went into effect on 1 April 1956 due to slippage of the F-104A operational debut, which caused TAC to alter its original plan, and by ADC's urgent need for a fighter-interceptor to fill the void between the F-102 and F-106. Also on 1 April 1956, the USAF decided that the F-104A Starfighter would be armed with two wingtip-mounted air-to-air, heat-

seeking AIM-9B Sidewinder missiles (one on either wingtip). Although the F-104A was never intended for use as an interceptor, its fantastic climb rate—35,000fpm—made ADC favor its interim use.

The USAF, specifically its ADC, accepted a total of 170 production F-104As, not 722 as originally planned in 1957. Shortages of funds, due to other aircraft programs, accounted for most of the reduction, while TAC's decision not to acquire the F-104A explained the remainder. Seven F-104As were accepted in fiscal year (FY) 1956, twenty-eight in FY 1957, ninety-four in FY 1958, and forty-

An F-104A begins its landing rollout at Edwards AFB. Speed brakes and both its leading- and trailing-edge flaps are *deployed; pilot chute has just begun to pull out the main braking chute. Lockheed via Campbell Archives*

one in FY 1959. One or two were accepted per month until May 1957; the delivery rate was slowed by development problems, but this later increased to four to eight per month as problems were cured. The final eight F-104As were delivered in December 1958. The average flyaway cost of each production F-104A was $1,704,228—that is, $1,026,859 for the airframe, $624,727 for the engine (installed), $3,419 for avionics, $29,517 for ordnance, and $19,706 for armament.

After the Lockheed F-104A had completed its testing at the Flight Test Center at Edwards AFB, the confidence of its designers was justified. More important, the USAF had grown to highly appreciate its new and advanced fighter plane, and it wanted the plane in its squadrons.

In the past, supersonic fighters had missed their estimates on performance and drag. Not so with the F-104A. It exceeded its drag and speed

requirements by two to three percent. Furthermore, its landing speed, with its boundary layer control system operating, was only five percent higher than older-type fighters. The simplicity of the design paid off. The Starfighter, even with its fantastic performance, cost about half as much as other fighters of the era. Additionally, the accessibility of system components was particularly appreciated and projected maintenance costs were favorable.

Pilot of an F-104A has just launched both wingtip-mounted AIM-9 Sidewinder missiles. The missiles' rocket motors have not yet ignited. Lockheed via Campbell Archives

YF-104A number fifteen takes off for delivery to USAF Aerospace Defense Command after

being brought up to F-104A standard for front-line service. Lockheed

To procure the Starfighter, the US Air Force placed its first order for 146 production F-104As—$100 million worth—on 14 October 1955. Even at this early milestone in the life of the Starfighter, the flexibility of the original F-104 design was apparent. Lockheed continued to work closely with the USAF to create additional versions of the aircraft that would be capable of other operational duties.

The Air Defense Command, which was renamed the USAF Aerospace

Defense Command and was responsible for safeguarding the United States against air attack, first assigned F-104As to its squadrons on 6 December 1956. The first ADC squadron to get the F-104A, the 83rd Fighter Interceptor Squadron (FIS) at Hamilton AFB, California, received its first batch of F-104As on 26 January 1958; the 83rd FIS became operational on 20 February. Due to the series of J79-GE-3/-3A engine malfunctions as discussed earlier, however, the 83rd FIS's new fighters were soon grounded. Fortunately the grounding was lifted as

soon as the more reliable J79-GE-3B engine began replacing the two earlier versions.

Use of the single-seat F-104A in the air defense role had been dictated by the slow arrival of the planned Convair F-106 Delta Dart. The USAF planned on having the F-106 in service in 1954, but it did not happen. Instead, F-104As had to be employed within ADC on an interim basis until the F-106 could be readily employed—some five years later than planned, in late 1959.

Two F-104As of the 83rd Fighter Interceptor Squadron (FIS) from Hamilton AFB, California, shortly after the type's initial *operational capability (IOC) had been achieved.* Lockheed

In addition to the 83rd FIS, three other Aerospace Defense Command squadrons—the 56th FIS (Wright-Patterson AFB, Ohio), 337th FIS (Westover AFB, Massachusetts), and 538th FIS (Larson AFB, Washington)—received the F-104A to use on an interim basis. Then in 1960, when the longer endurance, more heavily armed all-weather McDonnell F-101B Voodoos and

F-106As had entered service, Aerospace Defense Command transferred their F-104As to three Air National Guard (ANG) squadrons: the 151st FIS (Tennessee ANG), the 157th FIS (North Carolina ANG), and the 197th FIS (Arizona ANG). Thus, F-104As had been completely phased out of front-line service by late 1960.

F-104A Deployments and Phaseouts

In October 1958, twelve F-104As of the 83rd FIS were crated and airlifted by USAF Douglas C-124 Globemasters to Taiwan to serve temporarily with the Taiwanese air force during the Quemoy crisis. This was the F-104A's only deployment before its late 1960 phaseout.

A pair of 83rd FIS Starfighters over the Bay Bridge linking San Francisco with Oakland in California. Lockheed via Campbell Archives

Two 83rd FIS F-104As depart Hamilton AFB, California, on a training sortie. USAF via Campbell Archives

But when the Berlin crisis erupted in October 1961, the three ANG F-104A squadrons were called up for deployment to Europe. They deployed on 1 November 1961. Before their return to the United States, they deployed to Spain and Germany. The 157st FIS went to Moron, Spain, and both the 151st and 197th went to Ramstein AFB, Germany. These squadrons served in Europe until June 1962. Two ANG squadrons went back to duty with the Aerospace Defense Command, however, because of the Cuban Missile Crisis of October 1962. The third ANG squadron converted to flying Boeing C-97 Stratofreighters, and its F-104As were absorbed by the two new ADC squadrons—the 319th FIS (Homestead AFB, Florida) and the 331st FIS (Webb AFB, Texas). Surprisingly, these ADC squadrons traded in their all-weather F-102s and F-106s for daytime-only Starfighters. When the 319th FIS was disbanded in December 1969, their F-104A aircraft were completely phased out of front-line USAF service; the 331st FIS's F-104As had been completely phased out earlier. This was the *final* F-104A phaseout.

Foreign Service and Modified F-104As

Of the 170 production F-104A aircraft built, three were modified as NF-104A aerospace pilot trainers (serial numbers 56-756, -760, and -762). One went to the Royal Canadian Air Force as the prototype for the Canadian Starfighter, three went to NASA as F-104Ns (serial numbers 56-734, -749, and -790), ten went to the Pakistani air force, thirty-two went to the Jordanian air force, at least twenty-five went to the Taiwanese air force, and a minimum of seven F-104As were modified as remote-controlled QF-104A target drones in 1960. The remainder, those that had not been lost to attrition, went to the Aerospace Maintenance and Regeneration Center (AMARC) at Davis-Monthan AFB, Arizona.

The QF-104A Target Drone

In 1960, twenty-four YF-104A and F-104A aircraft (ratio unclear) were modified to serve as radio-controlled target drones, purposely shot down by friendly gun- , cannon- , and missile-firing fighters during armaments tests. As Lockheed TDN CL-396, these two dozen QF-104As could be flown by onboard

A lone, clean F-104A perched high above the clouds. USAF via Campbell Archives

pilots, pilots with remote-control from other aircraft, and pilots on the ground with radio-control equipment. The only known USAF squadron to operate these aircraft was the 3205th Drone Squadron at Eglin AFB, Florida, during the 1960s; flyaway cost per drone reached $1.7 million.

YF/F-104A Specifications

Crew	One
Wingspan	21.94ft (without wingtip fuel tanks)
Wing area	196.10sq-ft
Length	54.77ft
Height	13.49ft
Empty weight	12,780lb
Gross weight	17,770lb
Maximum speed	Mach 2.23 (attained)
Armament	One 20mm M61A1 Vulcan cannon; two AIM-9 Sidewinder missiles
Powerplant	One General Electric J79-GE-3/-3A/-3B/-11A/-19
Number built	170 (seventeen YF-104As, seven preproduction F-104As, and 146 production F-104As)

An F-104A at Mojave Airport, near Edwards AFB, being prepared for its modification into a QF-104A target drone. Gary James Collection

A QF-104A target drone; formerly YF-104A number twelve. USAF via Marty Isham

MAXIMUM GLIDE DISTANCE

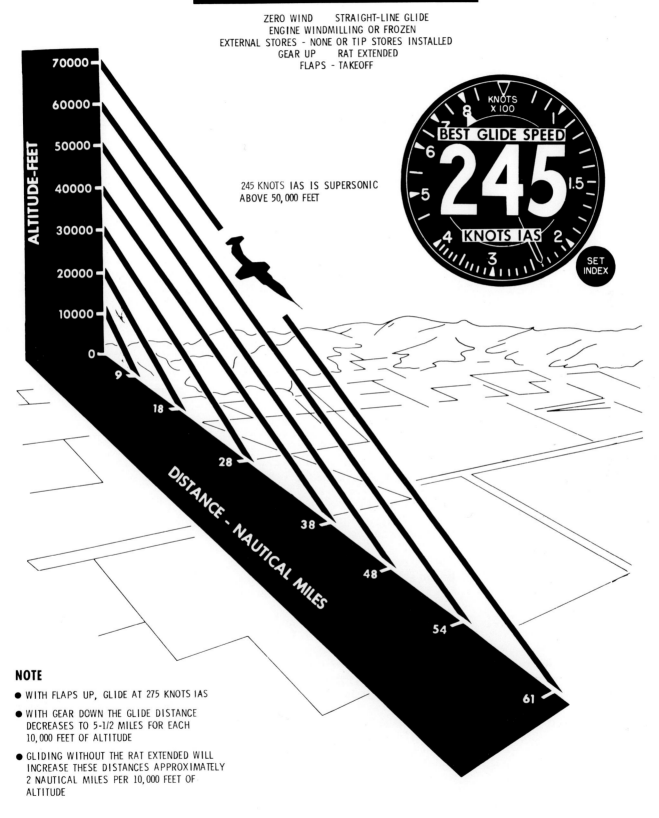

ZERO WIND   STRAIGHT-LINE GLIDE
ENGINE WINDMILLING OR FROZEN
EXTERNAL STORES - NONE OR TIP STORES INSTALLED
GEAR UP   RAT EXTENDED
FLAPS - TAKEOFF

245 KNOTS IAS IS SUPERSONIC
ABOVE 50,000 FEET

KNOTS X 100

BEST GLIDE SPEED
245
KNOTS IAS

SET INDEX

ALTITUDE-FEET

70000
60000
50000
40000
30000
20000
10000
0

DISTANCE - NAUTICAL MILES

9
18
28
38
48
54
61

NOTE

- WITH FLAPS UP, GLIDE AT 275 KNOTS IAS

- WITH GEAR DOWN THE GLIDE DISTANCE DECREASES TO 5-1/2 MILES FOR EACH 10,000 FEET OF ALTITUDE

- GLIDING WITHOUT THE RAT EXTENDED WILL INCREASE THESE DISTANCES APPROXIMATELY 2 NAUTICAL MILES PER 10,000 FEET OF ALTITUDE

Chapter 3

The F-104B Tandem-Seat Starfighter

Seven different USAF Century Series fighter aircraft made their respective first flights between the spring of 1953 and the winter of 1956, and, each was fully capable of flying at supersonic speed. During this era, the USAF Air Training Command was equipped with a subsonic primary jet trainer plane, the Lockheed T-33. With the advent of these seven supersonic fighters, including the F-104 Starfighter, the Air Training Command needed a supersonic primary jet trainer plane—and soon.

While it is true that the USAF had already ordered a dedicated supersonic primary jet trainer in June 1956, the Northrop T-38 Talon, it would not be available for some time. Lockheed, of course, knew this. Therefore, in late 1955, it proposed a tandem-seat derivative of its F-104A to serve as an interim supersonic primary jet trainer until the T-38 arrived. By 1957, the Air Force had ordered as many as 118 F-104Bs.

The USAF went along with Lockheed's proposal, and on 2 March 1956, placed an initial order for six tandem-seat Starfighters designated F-104B. These aircraft would be manufactured on the F-104A production line at Burbank. But, as planned, the first example was literally built by hand out of an F-104A airframe at Lockheed's facility at Palmdale, California. It was then trucked to Edwards for its first flight, which occurred on 16 January 1957. For a short time, this first example was classified as a service test aircraft—thus, it was unofficially designated YF-104B. But, since it was never officially designated as such, it will be referred to as F-104B number one.

Thirteen days before its first flight, on 3 January 1957, a USAF Flight Test Center directive advised that "the AFFTC will conduct a limited Phase II test program on the service test F-104B in February 1957. A limited Phase IV test program will be conducted on the number three production F-104B in December 1957."

The F-104B

The only external configuration changes between the one-seat F-104A and the two-seat F-104B was the B-model's longer canopy to cover two cockpits, and the twenty-five percent larger vertical stabilizer. To create the F-104B, and to provide space for the second cockpit, Lockheed removed the 20mm cannon, relocated various avionics, installed an aftward-retracting nose landing gear (as used on the two XF-104s), and reduced the internal fuel capacity from 897 to 752 gallons. The provision for two wingtip and two underwing external fuel tanks was retained. This increased the B's total fuel capacity to 1,482 gallons. The F-104B could be armed with two wingtip-mounted AIM-9 Sidewinders and retained the AN/ASG-14T-1 fire control system.

The F-104B was assigned to tactical organizations at the rate of four per squadron for pilot transition and, if required, they could be used for tactical operations.

Following Lockheed's Phase I and Phase III tests on the number one F-104B at Edwards AFB, the USAF conducted a ten-flight Phase II test program at Lockheed's Palmdale facility between 29 May and 20 June 1957; Phase II flying time was six hours and twenty minutes. The purpose of the Phase II test, according to the USAF, was "to find any deficiencies in the aircraft and to compare its characteristics to those of the F-104A within the present [spring 1957] operating limits of Mach 1.7 for the small vertical fin which has to be installed on F-104B number one as yet." Production F-104Bs were fitted with the larger area vertical tail and, like all earlier and subsequent Starfighters, incorporated powered rudders.

Upon completion of the USAF Phase II test program on the first F-104B, the USAF evaluated the plane as follows:

The performance of the F-104B is almost identical to that of the F-104A; however, the reduced internal fuel capacity severely limits the usefulness of the aircraft. External fuel tanks should be considered as the normal loading of the aircraft for training and weather flights.

Stability characteristics are satisfactory within the limits observed during these tests, and closely approximate those of the F-104A. Control forces are considered high during maneuvering flight and exceed the maximum specified limit.

Although the general layout of and visibility from both cockpits are excellent, there are numerous discrepancies in both cockpits which are distracting and unsatisfactory. The red color of some warning lights is in violation of the *Handbook for Aircraft Design*.

With the discrepancies corrected, and with external fuel tanks installed, the production F-104B should be an excellent trainer. It will also fulfill the same tactical mission as the F-104A within the limitations of reduced range and endurance caused by the reduced internal fuel capacity.

The larger area vertical tail, the boundary layer control system, the automatic pitch control system, and the armament and fire control system were not installed in F-104B number one.

During the USAF Phase II test on F-104B number one, test pilots found that its handling characteristics on the ground were good and similar to the F-104A (YF-104A number one was used for the comparison). Takeoff characteristics were similar to the F-104A except that rudder kicks were introduced occasionally by the nose wheel steering system during gear retraction.

Acceleration performance at 35,000ft with maximum power was identical to the F-104A. The USAF noted:

Acceleration through Mach 1 to 1.05 was good, but acceleration from Mach 1.05 to near 1.3 was relatively slow, reaching a minimum of Mach 1.175. From Mach 1.175, the acceleration increased steadily to Mach 1.6 where it was excellent and then it decreased slightly before reaching Mach 1.7, the limit of these tests.

The USAF Phase IV tests on production F-104B number three began in

December 1957 as planned; these concluded after some thirty hours in January 1958.

Earlier, on 4 December 1956, a contract for twenty additional production F-104Bs was approved. This brought total procurement of the type up to twenty-six, counting the service test F-104B, which was later brought up to F-104B standards. The first production F-104B was delivered in September 1957, the last in November 1958. All F-104Bs were either powered by

An F-104B at McClellan AFB, California, at the Air Logistics Center, circa 1971. F-104D *style cockpit canopy is of interest.* Marty Isham

41

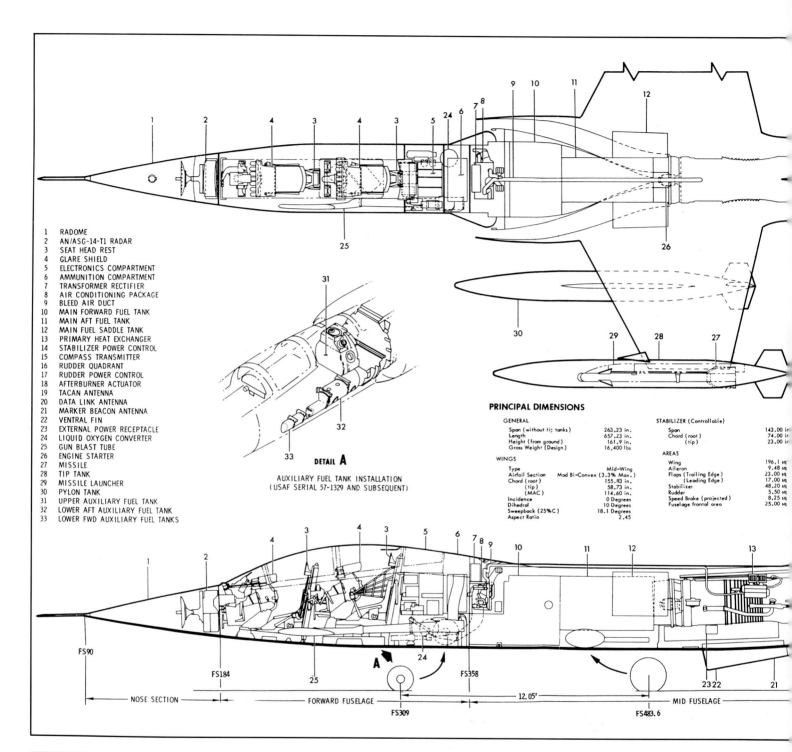

1. RADOME
2. AN/ASG-14-T1 RADAR
3. SEAT HEAD REST
4. GLARE SHIELD
5. ELECTRONICS COMPARTMENT
6. AMMUNITION COMPARTMENT
7. TRANSFORMER RECTIFIER
8. AIR CONDITIONING PACKAGE
9. BLEED AIR DUCT
10. MAIN FORWARD FUEL TANK
11. MAIN AFT FUEL TANK
12. MAIN FUEL SADDLE TANK
13. PRIMARY HEAT EXCHANGER
14. STABILIZER POWER CONTROL
15. COMPASS TRANSMITTER
16. RUDDER QUADRANT
17. RUDDER POWER CONTROL
18. AFTERBURNER ACTUATOR
19. TACAN ANTENNA
20. DATA LINK ANTENNA
21. MARKER BEACON ANTENNA
22. VENTRAL FIN
23. EXTERNAL POWER RECEPTACLE
24. LIQUID OXYGEN CONVERTER
25. GUN BLAST TUBE
26. ENGINE STARTER
27. MISSILE
28. TIP TANK
29. MISSILE LAUNCHER
30. PYLON TANK
31. UPPER AUXILIARY FUEL TANK
32. LOWER AFT AUXILIARY FUEL TANK
33. LOWER FWD AUXILIARY FUEL TANKS

DETAIL A

AUXILIARY FUEL TANK INSTALLATION
(USAF SERIAL 57-1329 AND SUBSEQUENT)

PRINCIPAL DIMENSIONS

GENERAL

Span (without tip tanks)	263.23 in.
Length	657.23 in.
Height (from ground)	161.9 in.
Gross Weight (Design)	16,400 lbs

WINGS

Type	Mid-Wing
Airfoil Section	Mod Bi-Convex (3.3% Max.)
Chord (root)	155.83 in.
(tip)	58.73 in.
(MAC)	114.60 in.
Incidence	0 Degrees
Dihedral	10 Degrees
Sweepback (25%C)	18.1 Degrees
Aspect Ratio	2.45

STABILIZER (Controllable)

Span	143.00 in
Chord (root)	74.00 in
(tip)	23.00 in

AREAS

Wing	196.1 sq
Aileron	9.48 sq
Flaps (Trailing Edge)	23.00 sq
(Leading Edge)	17.00 sq
Stabilizer	48.20 sq
Rudder	5.50 sq
Speed Brake (projected)	8.25 sq
Fuselage frontal area	25.00 sq

FS90
FS184
NOSE SECTION
FORWARD FUSELAGE
FS309
A
FS358
12.05'
FS483.6
MID FUSELAGE

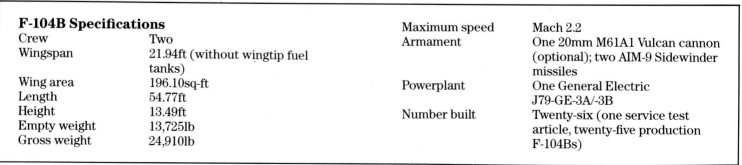

F-104B Specifications

Crew	Two	Maximum speed	Mach 2.2
Wingspan	21.94ft (without wingtip fuel tanks)	Armament	One 20mm M61A1 Vulcan cannon (optional); two AIM-9 Sidewinder missiles
Wing area	196.10sq-ft	Powerplant	One General Electric J79-GE-3A/-3B
Length	54.77ft		
Height	13.49ft	Number built	Twenty-six (one service test article, twenty-five production F-104Bs)
Empty weight	13,725lb		
Gross weight	24,910lb		

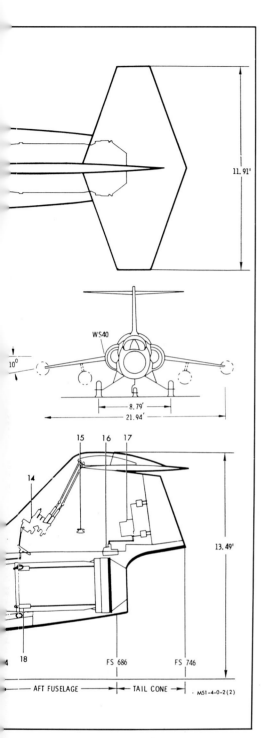

Inboard profile of an F-104B. Lockheed

F-104Bs and F-104As of the 151st FIS, Tennessee Air National Guard. Gary James Collection

the J79-GE-3A or the J79-GE-3B as engine improvements came about.

As had been proposed by Lockheed and approved by the USAF, provision was retained for the installation of the 20mm Vulcan cannon in the F-104B if it was required for tactical operation. By removing key segments of the aft cockpit (seat, and so on), the cannon and ammunition drum could be installed. In essence, the two-seat F-104B trainer would transform into a single-seat fighter-interceptor like the F-104A.

The F-104B Enters Service

The first recipient of the F-104B was the Air Defense Command's 83rd FIS at Hamilton AFB, California, in early 1958. Subsequently, all three F-104A squadrons received the aircraft. For its purpose,

NASA got one F-104B (serial number 57-1303).

The USAF accepted one F-104B in FY (fiscal year) 1957, fourteen more in FY 1958, and the last seven in FY 1959. The flyaway cost of each F-104B was $2,397,130—that is, $1,756,388 for the airframe, $336,015 for the engine (installed), $13,258 for avionics, $59,473 for ordnance, and $231,996 for armament.

As did the single-seat F-104As, the tandem-seat F-104Bs went through two phase-outs. First transferred to the Air National Guard in 1960, F-104Bs were returned to Air Defense Command's inventory during 1962 and 1963; and like the A-model, the B-model was phased out again during 1967–69. After this, F-104Bs went to Jordan and Taiwan; the remainder (unserviceables) went into storage at Davis-Monthan AFB, Arizona.

Chapter 4

The F-104C Tactical Strike Trainer

Although USAF Air Defense Command had badly needed a supersonic fighter-interceptor to fill the gap between the F-102 and F-106, Tactical Air Command also needed a supersonic tactical strike fighter (fighter-bomber) to fill the void between the forthcoming F-100C and the Republic F-105B Thunderchief. To this end then, on 2 March 1956, a contract was approved for an initial procurement of fifty-six F-104C tactical strike Starfighters; this amount was later

The first of seventy-seven F-104Cs produced for Tactical Air Command. This Starfighter went to the 436th Tactical Fighter Squadron (TFS) *of the 479th Tactical Fighter Wing* (TFW) *at George AFB, California.* Lockheed

increased to seventy-seven when a second order for twenty-one additional F-104Cs was approved on 26 December 1956.

The first F-104C (temporarily and unofficially designated YF-104C by the USAF) made its maiden flight on 24 July 1958. Much better than its A-model relative, the single-seat F-104C featured the all-up AN/ASG-14T-2 fire control system, a removable probe-and-drogue system for aerial refueling, and the ability to carry a single nuclear store (either a B28 nuclear bomb or a Douglas AIR-2 Genie air-to-air rocket), conventional bombs and unguided rockets in pods on underwing and fuselage pylons, auxiliary fuel tanks on underwing pylons, two additional AIM-9 Sidewinder air-to-air missiles on a pylon under the fuselage on centerline. Furthermore it came with the more reliable and higher thrust GE J79-GE-7A turbojet engine that delivered 10,000lb military thrust and 15,800lb afterburning thrust. But like the F-104A, the F-104C was only capable of daytime and clear nighttime operations.

The F-104C airframe, systems, and engine were more easily maintained than the same components on the F-104A. Tactical versatility and potential of the C-model Starfighter had been significantly increased by its in-flight refueling capability, the addition of two more air-to-air missiles, and provision for belly-mounted and underwing stores of a wide variety—conventional and nuclear. Moreover, after the improved M61A1

Four F-104Cs of the 479th TFW on a training mission out of George AFB. Note that USAF serial number 56-0908 is the only C-model here with its in-flight refueling probe attached. USAF via Robert F. Dorr

Vulcan appeared in 1964, the F-104C weapon system finally became complete.

During the time from 21 September to 21 November 1958, the limited Phase II tests were performed by the USAF at Edwards AFB.

The USAF Phase II tests were primarily designed to give a qualitative analysis of the differences between the F-104C and the F-104A, to determine the full potential of the M61 Vulcan cannon (still suffering from developmental problems), and to obtain an evaluation of the complete AN/ASG-14T-2 fire control system and the aircraft's in-flight refueling capability. An operable cannon, gunsight, pylons for external stores, and the production infrared sight were incorporated for these tests.

The first four F-104C aircraft produced were used in contractor Phase I and Phase III tests, and in USAF Phase II and Phase IV tests at Edwards AFB. After its early flight-test activities, the first F-104C arrived at Edwards on 17 September 1958 and engaged in eighty flights totaling eighty-six hours. It completed its last flight on 14 November. The second F-104C arrived on 19 September, engaged in seventy flights totaling eighty hours and fifty-five minutes, and it completed its final flight on 4 November. The third F-104C arrived on 23 September, performed seventy-eight flights adding up to seventy-eight hours and forty minutes, and completed

Four brand-new F-104Cs on their delivery flight to the 479th TFW. Lockheed

its final flight on 21 November. The fourth F-104C arrived on 20 September, performed seventy-three flights totaling sixty-six hours and thirty-five minutes, and completed its last flight on 21 November 1958. The cumulative flights of all four participating F-104C aircraft totaled 301, and total flight time was 312 hours and ten minutes. This was one of the most intense flight-test programs to date.

The number of flights for each type of mission was as follows: five high-altitude zoom flights, twenty J79-GE-7A engine evaluation flights, sixty-two pilot familiarization and requalification flights, twenty-nine Vulcan cannon free-fire flights, seventy-one air-to-air gunnery flights, twenty-two air-to-ground gunnery flights, fifteen tactics and technique flights, seventeen in-flight refueling exercises, eight infrared sight evaluations, and fifty-three miscellaneous—aborts, functional check flights, simulated flameouts, and so forth.

When completed, the USAF evaluated the F-104C as follows:

Within the scope of these tests, the F-104C is suitable for its assigned mission; however, improved aircraft utilization and mission effectiveness can be obtained by prompt correction of the following deficiencies: engine roughness at high rpm [revolutions per minute]; poor afterburner

A trio of F-104Cs with wingtip-mounted Sidewinders and attached-in-flight refueling probes. Lockheed

476th TFS Starfighters stop over at Lajes AB in the Azores en route to Germany. Ray Holt via Warren Thompson

light reliability; low service life of engine components; inadequate aircraft fuel quantity indication; and marginal radar component reliability.

During a low-key ceremony, the Tactical Air Command accepted the F-104C Starfighter on 15 October 1958 during the annual USAF Fighter Weapons Meet at Nellis AFB, Nevada. The 476th Tactical Fighter Squadron (TFS) of the 479th Tactical Fighter Wing (TFW) at George AFB, California, was first to

In-flight view of 476th TFS F-104s en route to Hahn AB in Germany. Ray Holt via Warren Thompson

One of the 476th's Starfighters in a revetment at Hahn. Ray Holt via Warren Thompson

receive the F-104C. And, subsequently, three other 479th TFW squadrons—the 434th, 435th, and 436th TFSs—received the F-104C—the *only* Tactical Air Command squadrons that did.

Seventy-seven F-104Cs were built. All were accepted during FY 1959, and were delivered at a rate of seven to nine per month. The average flyaway cost of each production F-104C was $1,478,402—that is, $863,235 for the airframe, $473,729 for the engine (installed), $5,219 for avionics, $44,684 for ordnance, and $91,535 for armament.

Ray Holt poses in the cockpit of his F-104 at Hahn in August 1962. Ray Holt via Warren Thompson

A 479th TFW weapons display at George AFB in May 1963. Ray Holt via Warren Thompson

The F-104C had a number of operational problems with various components (radar, cannon, and so on) as well as the J79-GE-7A engine, a major offender (forty serious mishaps occurring in under five years killing nine pilots and destroying twenty-four aircraft), which led to Project Seven

An F-104C over the battle zone during Exercise Desert Strike, a joint US Army and US Air Force Strike Command exercise carried out during 5–29 May 1964 on and over some 9,600 miles of the Mojave Desert in California. USAF via Robert F. Dorr

Mike Korte in the cockpit of his Starfighter in February 1974. Mike Korte via Warren Thompson

Up—a General Electric modification program on its -7A engine that began in May 1963 and ended in June 1964.

In early 1963, the USAF initiated Project Grindstone whereby Lockheed modified the F-104C so it could carry up to four AIM-9 Sidewinder air-to-air guided missiles for its secondary air defense role, and so it could carry a variety of tactical air-to-ground ordnance, including unguided high-explosive 2.75in diameter rockets, conventional and nuclear bombs, and napalm canisters.

Tactical Air Command phased out its F-104Cs in 1967, four years later than scheduled because they were needed to fight the Vietnam War. The C-model then joined the Puerto Rico Air National Guard, when the 198th TFS converted in August 1967 from the obsolete North American F-86H Sabre Jet.

F-104C (57-0916) of 479th TFW at Langley AFB, Virginia, circa 1988; ADC gray paint scheme is noteworthy. Gary James Collection

F-104C (56-0932) of Puerto Rico ANG's 198th TFS, circa 1977, before being replaced by A-7Ds. Photo taken at Van Nuys, California.
P. C. Hodgdon via Gary James Collection

Former F-104C of Puerto Rico ANG, circa 1990, at unknown location. The F-104C Starfighter could carry either two or four Sidewinders. For nuclear strike, a Mk28 store could be carried under the fuselage. Gary James Collection

F-104C Specifications

Crew	One
Wingspan	21.94ft (without wingtip fuel tanks)
Wing area	196.10sq-ft
Length	54.77ft
Height	13.49ft
Empty weight	12,760lb
Gross weight	27,850lb
Maximum speed	Mach 2.2
Armament	One 20mm M61A1 Vulcan cannon; four AIM-9 Sidewinder missiles; various conventional and nuclear ordnance
Powerplant	One General Electric J79-GE-7A
Number built	Seventy-seven

Former 151st FIS F-104C (56-0890) of Tennessee ANG, circa 1988, is now a gate guardian at Knoxville, Tennessee. Paul Biglow via Gary James Collection

Chapter 5

The F-104D Tactical Strike Trainer

Much the same as the Air Defense Command needed a tandem-seat trainer version of the single-seat F-104A, Tactical Air Command required a trainer derivative of the F-104C. And, much like the B-model was a dual-seat A-model, the D-model was a two-seat C-model.

The F-104D was the last version of the Starfighter procured by the USAF. Tactical Air Command accepted twenty-one F-104Ds between November 1958 and September 1959. The first example was flight-tested on 31 October 1958—by chance, exactly six years after Kelly Johnson had proposed TDN L-246 to

Tandem-seat F-104D shows revised cockpit canopies and in-flight refueling probe. Back seat is higher than front seat for forward visibility from aft cockpit. Lockheed

Lockheed management for its consideration.

Like the B-model featured the refinements of the A-model, the D-model sported the improvements of the C-model. And, like the B-model, the D-model incorporated the larger area vertical fin. The D-model's two-part cockpit canopy was strengthened. The F-104D had in-flight refueling capability like the F-104C, it was powered by the same engine (J79-GE-7A), and carried the same armament (installation of the Vulcan cannon was optional). Moreover, the D's nose landing gear retracted aftward like the B's.

The first Tactical Air Command unit to get the F-104D was the 476th TFS at George AFB. This occurred in November 1958, and subsequently, Tactical Air Command's three other F-104C squadrons assigned to the 479th TFW at George AFB—the 434th, 435th, and 436th TFSs—received F-104Ds.

The flyaway cost of each production F-104D airplane was $1,500,391—that is, $873,952 for the airframe, $271,148 for the engine (installed), $16,210 for avionics, $70,067 for ordnance, and $269,014 for armament.

The F-104D, like the F-104C, was phased out of regular USAF service in 1967; it likewise went to the 198th TFS in the Puerto Rico Air National Guard.

This F-104D of the 479th TFW crashed at Tinker AFB, Oklahoma, on 22 May 1961. The aircraft was repaired to soldier on. USAF via Campbell Archives

The tandem-seat F-104D was exactly the same length as the single-seat F-104C but still had two cockpits. Peter Wilson via Gary James Collection

F-104D Specifications

Crew	Two
Wingspan	21.94ft (without wingtip fuel tanks)
Wing area	196.10sq-ft
Length	54.77ft
Height	13.49ft
Empty weight	13,725lb
Gross weight	24,910lb
Maximum speed	Mach 2.2
Armament	One 20mm M61A1 Vulcan cannon (optional); two AIM-9 Sidewinder missiles; various conventional and nuclear ordnance
Powerplant	One General Electric J79-GE-7A
Number built	Twenty-one

Puerto Rico Air National Guard F-104D, circa 1974, in Southeast Asia camouflage dress. Gary James Collection

Chapter 6

Structures and Systems

Lockheed's F-104 Starfighter, in its numerous domestic and foreign guises, employed a number of structures and systems to meet its ever-changing mission and user requirements. Originally designed as an air superiority day fighter, the F-104 filled many missions over the years: daytime fighter-interceptor, fighter-bomber, fighter-trainer, photographic reconnaissance aircraft, and all-weather, multi-role fighter.

What had once been a light, fast, quick-climbing fighter became an ordnance-laden platform—a beast of burden. But once it was able to off-load its backbreaking external fuel tanks, missiles, rockets, and bombs, the F-104 transformed into the air combat fighter that Kelly Johnson and the Korean War fighter pilots envisaged in 1951—an authentic star fighter. But, as capable as the F-104 was for air combat (Johnson believed it could have beat the McDonnell Douglas F-15 Eagle in a dogfight), the Starfighter had been overtaken by the technologies it helped create—the price of aviation progress.

Fuselage Structures

All versions of the F-104 have all-metal monocoque fuselage structures, fabricated primarily from aluminum alloy. The aft fuselage structure is fabricated from titanium alloy because the J79 turbojet engine's afterburner produces extreme temperatures. The fuselage has hydraulically operated aluminum alloy speed brakes on either side of the aft fuselage.

Wing Structures

The F-104 incorporates a cantilever mid-wing configuration. The wing is of

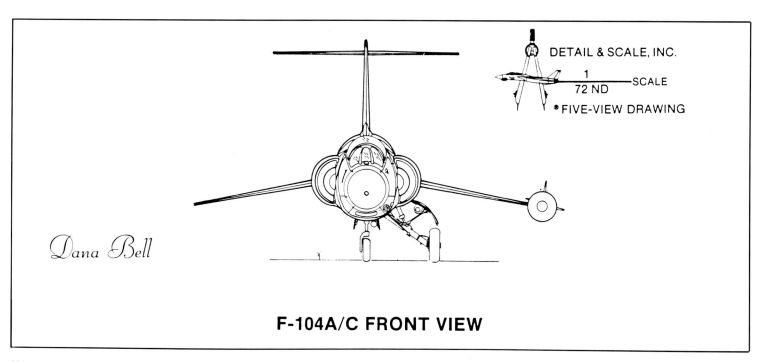

DETAIL & SCALE, INC.

$\frac{1}{72 \text{ ND}}$ SCALE

® FIVE-VIEW DRAWING

Dana Bell

F-104A/C FRONT VIEW

Next pages
Detail & Scale, Inc. ¹/₇₂nd scale five-view drawing of F-104A/C and F-104B/D

Starfighter aircraft by Dana Bell. Detail & Scale, Inc.

the bi-convex supersonic airfoil section with a thickness-to-chord ratio of 3.36 percent. It has a dihedral of minus-ten degrees (downward angle) with zero incidence. The wing has a leading-edge radius of 0.016in, which is not exactly razor-sharp, but the trailing edge does taper to a razor-sharp apex. It sweeps back eighteen degrees six minutes at the quarter-chord, and each half-wing measures just 7ft, 7in from root to tip.

The F-104 wing is of all-metal aluminum alloy construction with two main spars, twelve spanwise intermediate channels between spars, and upper and lower one-piece skin panels that taper from a thickness of 0.25in at the wing root to 0.125in at the wingtip. Each half-wing is a separate structure supported by five forged frames in the fuselage. The half-wings have full-span, electrically actuated leading edge slats. Their entire trailing edges are hinged, with inboard sections serving as landing flaps and outboard sections as ailerons.

The ailerons are aluminum alloy, each powered by a servo control system that is hydraulically powered, each actuated by ten small hydraulic cylinders. Trim control is applied to position the aileron relative to the servo control position; an electric actuator positions the aileron trim.

The flaps are aluminum alloy and electrically actuated. Above each flap is the air-delivery tube of a boundary layer control system, which ejects air that has been bled from the engine compressor over the entire flap span when the flaps are lowered to the landing configuration.

Tail Structures

The F-104 has a cantilever T-tail structure and all-flying, one-piece horizontal tail surfaces that are hinged at the mid-chord point atop the vertical fin and are powered by hydraulic servos. The

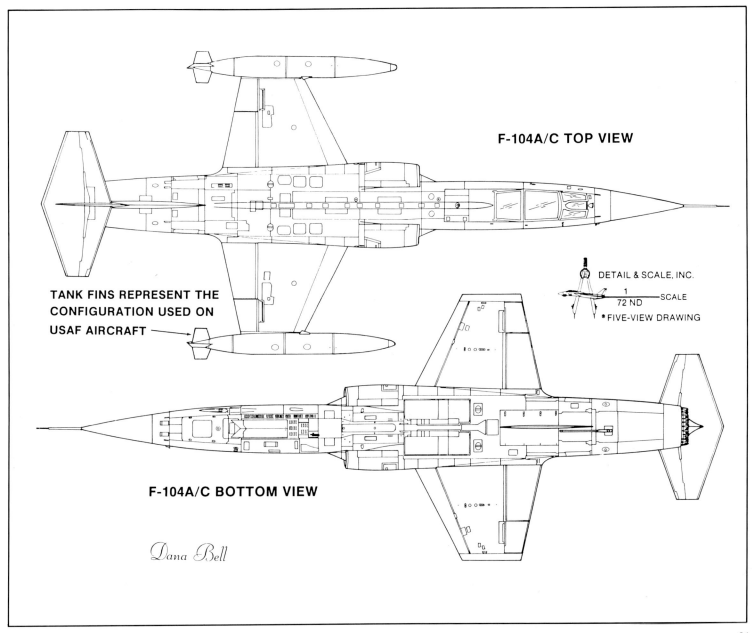

F-104A/C TOP VIEW

TANK FINS REPRESENT THE CONFIGURATION USED ON USAF AIRCRAFT →

DETAIL & SCALE, INC.

1 / 72 ND — SCALE

• FIVE-VIEW DRAWING

F-104A/C BOTTOM VIEW

Dana Bell

horizontal stabilator (combined stabilizer and elevator) has a profile similar to the wing and is constructed of aluminum alloy.

The rudder is fully powered by a hydraulic servo; trim control is applied to position the tailplane relative to the servo control position via an electric actuator. Rudder trim is operated by an electric actuator inside the vertical fin. The rudder itself is trimmed in the same way as the stabilator.

All F-104s have a narrow-chord ventral fin on centerline; however, the Fiat-built Lockheed F-104S also has two smaller lateral fins under the fuselage to further improve high-speed, high-altitude stability.

Landing Gear and Braking Systems

The F-104 has a hydraulically actuated tricycle landing gear arrangement with Dowty-patented liquid-spring shock absorbers. The main landing gear retracts forward and upward into the fuselage. The steerable nose landing gear retracts forward and upward into the fuselage on one-place aircraft and aftward and upward on two-place F-104s. The main landing gear legs are hinged on oblique axes so the wheels and tires will lay flat within the fuselage after retraction.

For braking, the F-104 has hydraulic Bendix disc brakes with Goodyear anti-skid units. A large eighteen-foot-diameter braking parachute is employed from its compartment under the aft fuselage. An

arrester hook is also employed under the aft fuselage, forward of the parachute housing.

Goodrich tires are used: Type VII for nosewheel, Type VIII for main wheels. Respectively, the sizes are 18.0x5.5in and 26.0x8.0in. The wheel track is 8ft 10³/₄in, wheelbase is 15ft ¹/₂in.

Accommodation

All F-104 cockpits were fully pressurized and air-conditioned for pilot comfort, with canopies that open to port for pilot entries and exits. Different styles of cockpit canopies were incorporated on tandem-seat Starfighters. The F-104B had a one-piece metal frame between the two canopies, while the F-104D had a solid metal-framed transparency between the two canopies. The F-104F,

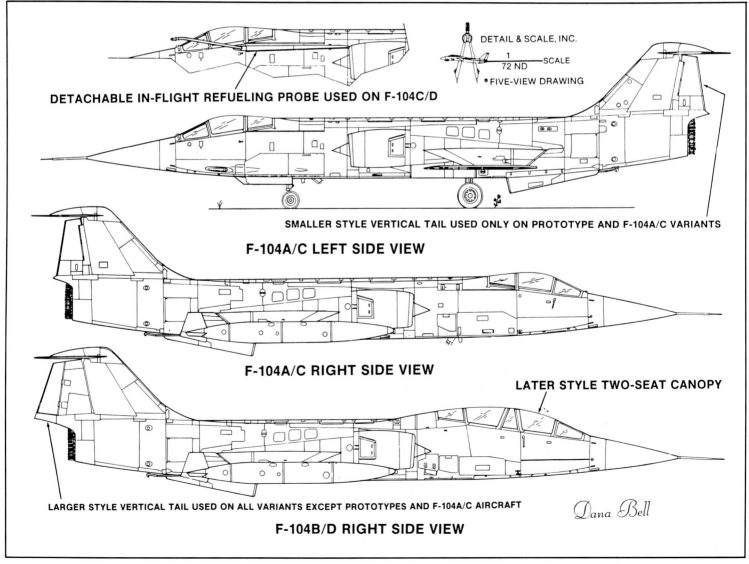

DETACHABLE IN-FLIGHT REFUELING PROBE USED ON F-104C/D

DETAIL & SCALE, INC.

1
72 ND ── SCALE

FIVE-VIEW DRAWING

SMALLER STYLE VERTICAL TAIL USED ONLY ON PROTOTYPE AND F-104A/C VARIANTS

F-104A/C LEFT SIDE VIEW

F-104A/C RIGHT SIDE VIEW

LATER STYLE TWO-SEAT CANOPY

LARGER STYLE VERTICAL TAIL USED ON ALL VARIANTS EXCEPT PROTOTYPES AND F-104A/C AIRCRAFT

Dana Bell

F-104B/D RIGHT SIDE VIEW

CF-104D, F-104DJ, and TF-104G tandem-seat aircraft all used the latter style.

Emergency Ejection Seat System

Three different emergency ejection seat systems have been incorporated in the F-104, one downward-firing and two upward-firing. All systems employed rocket propulsion for seat ejection from the aircraft. Two systems—one downward-firing and one upward-firing—were developed by Lockheed. The third system—developed by Martin-Baker—is upward-firing.

Downward-Firing System

When the F-104 was first designed, Lockheed engineers feared that an upward-firing emergency ejection seat system would not be safe. They believed that upward ejections at the speeds the aircraft would fly would contribute to severe pilot injuries or deaths—that is, their seats would not have time to clear the aircraft's tail group safely at supersonic speeds. Thus, they developed a downward-firing system. As it turned out, however, the downward-firing system proved more dangerous because it could not be used during takeoffs, landings, or anywhere near the ground. In fact, if a pilot had to eject at low altitude, he would have to roll the aircraft inverted (upside down), then eject upward out the bottom of the plane. Worse, during takeoff and landing maneuvers, the pilot would be forced to eject straight into the ground or

stay with the aircraft if an emergency arose.

When new, the F-104's downward-firing ejection seat system was called unique. It was the first fully automatic, downward-firing system ever employed in a production fighter plane. Although it was unpopular with Starfighter pilots from the outset and later replaced with upward-firing systems, the downward-firing system worked as follows: after the ejection ring was pulled, (1) the cockpit depressurized and the flight control stick stowed away; (2) the parachute shoulder harness tightened, and the pilot's feet were pulled together and clamped into place; (3) explosive bolts blew the escape hatch off the bottom of the plane, and the

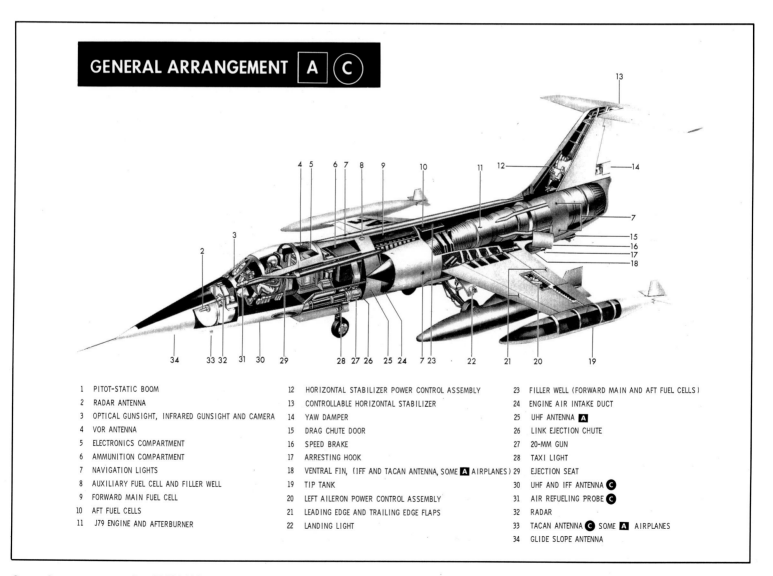

GENERAL ARRANGEMENT A C

1	PITOT-STATIC BOOM	12	HORIZONTAL STABILIZER POWER CONTROL ASSEMBLY	23	FILLER WELL (FORWARD MAIN AND AFT FUEL CELLS)
2	RADAR ANTENNA	13	CONTROLLABLE HORIZONTAL STABILIZER	24	ENGINE AIR INTAKE DUCT
3	OPTICAL GUNSIGHT, INFRARED GUNSIGHT AND CAMERA	14	YAW DAMPER	25	UHF ANTENNA A
4	VOR ANTENNA	15	DRAG CHUTE DOOR	26	LINK EJECTION CHUTE
5	ELECTRONICS COMPARTMENT	16	SPEED BRAKE	27	20-MM GUN
6	AMMUNITION COMPARTMENT	17	ARRESTING HOOK	28	TAXI LIGHT
7	NAVIGATION LIGHTS	18	VENTRAL FIN, (IFF AND TACAN ANTENNA, SOME A AIRPLANES)	29	EJECTION SEAT
8	AUXILIARY FUEL CELL AND FILLER WELL	19	TIP TANK	30	UHF AND IFF ANTENNA C
9	FORWARD MAIN FUEL CELL	20	LEFT AILERON POWER CONTROL ASSEMBLY	31	AIR REFUELING PROBE C
10	AFT FUEL CELLS	21	LEADING EDGE AND TRAILING EDGE FLAPS	32	RADAR
11	J79 ENGINE AND AFTERBURNER	22	LANDING LIGHT	33	TACAN ANTENNA C SOME A AIRPLANES
				34	GLIDE SLOPE ANTENNA

General arrangement of an F-104A/C.
Lockheed

Structural view of an F-104B. Lockheed

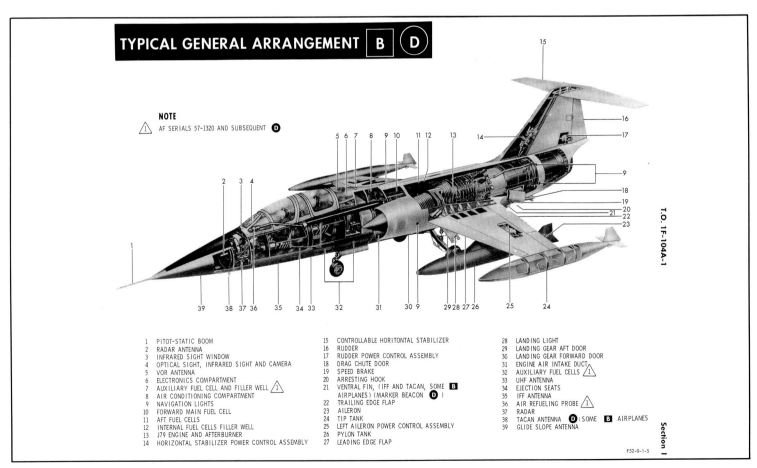

TYPICAL GENERAL ARRANGEMENT [B] (D)

NOTE

△1 AF SERIALS 57-1320 AND SUBSEQUENT (D)

T.O. 1F-104A-1

1	PITOT-STATIC BOOM	15	CONTROLLABLE HORITONTAL STABILIZER	28	LANDING LIGHT		
2	RADAR ANTENNA	16	RUDDER	29	LANDING GEAR AFT DOOR		
3	INFRARED SIGHT WINDOW	17	RUDDER POWER CONTROL ASSEMBLY	30	LANDING GEAR FORWARD DOOR		
4	OPTICAL SIGHT, INFRARED SIGHT AND CAMERA	18	DRAG CHUTE DOOR	31	ENGINE AIR INTAKE DUCT △1		
5	VOR ANTENNA	19	SPEED BRAKE	32	AUXILIARY FUEL CELLS △1		
6	ELECTRONICS COMPARTMENT	20	ARRESTING HOOK	33	UHF ANTENNA		
7	AUXILIARY FUEL CELL AND FILLER WELL △1	21	VENTRAL FIN, (IFF AND TACAN, SOME [B]	34	EJECTION SEATS		
8	AIR CONDITIONING COMPARTMENT		AIRPLANES) (MARKER BEACON (D))	35	IFF ANTENNA		
9	NAVIGATION LIGHTS	22	TRAILING EDGE FLAP	36	AIR REFUELING PROBE △1		
10	FORWARD MAIN FUEL CELL	23	AILERON	37	RADAR		
11	AFT. FUEL CELLS	24	TIP TANK	38	TACAN ANTENNA (D) :SOME [B] AIRPLANES		
12	INTERNAL FUEL CELLS FILLER WELL	25	LEFT AILERON POWER CONTROL ASSEMBLY	39	GLIDE SLOPE ANTENNA		
13	J79 ENGINE AND AFTERBURNER	26	PYLON TANK				
14	HORIZONTAL STABILIZER POWER CONTROL ASSEMBLY	27	LEADING EDGE FLAP				

Section I

F52-0-1-5

The general arrangement drawing from the
Air Force manual. USAF via James C. Goodall

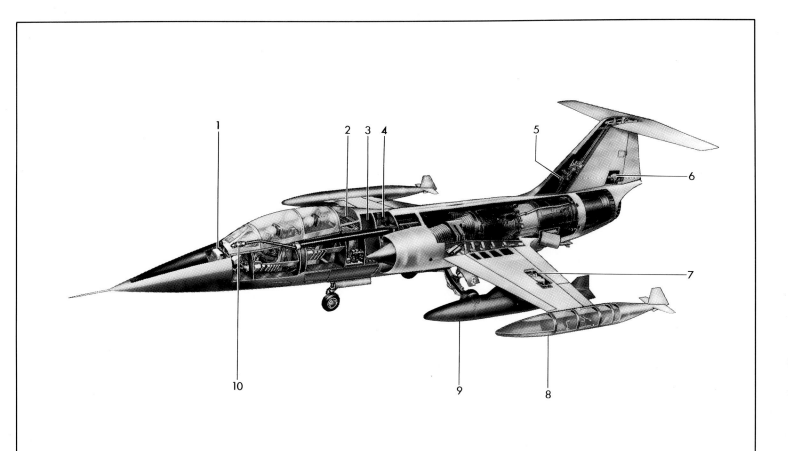

1	RADAR
2	FORWARD ELECTRONICS COMPARTMENT
3	AFT ELECTRONICS COMPARTMENT
4	AIR CONDITIONING PACKAGE
5	STABILIZER POWER CONTROL ASSEMBLY
6	RUDDER POWER CONTROL ASSEMBLY
7	AILERON POWER CONTROL ASSEMBLY
8	TIP TANK
9	PYLON TANK
10	AERIAL REFUELING PROBE

Cutaway view of an F-104D. Lockheed

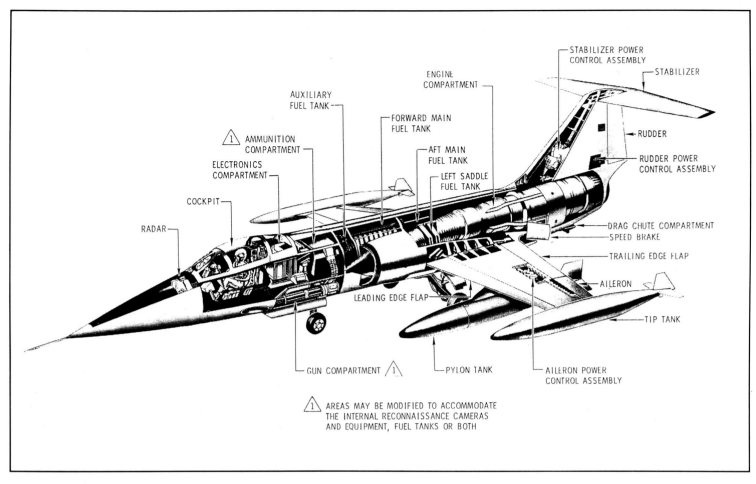

STABILIZER POWER CONTROL ASSEMBLY
STABILIZER
ENGINE COMPARTMENT
AUXILIARY FUEL TANK
FORWARD MAIN FUEL TANK
RUDDER
AFT MAIN FUEL TANK
RUDDER POWER CONTROL ASSEMBLY
△1 AMMUNITION COMPARTMENT
ELECTRONICS COMPARTMENT
LEFT SADDLE FUEL TANK
COCKPIT
DRAG CHUTE COMPARTMENT
SPEED BRAKE
RADAR
TRAILING EDGE FLAP
AILERON
LEADING EDGE FLAP
TIP TANK
GUN COMPARTMENT △1
PYLON TANK
AILERON POWER CONTROL ASSEMBLY
△1 AREAS MAY BE MODIFIED TO ACCOMMODATE THE INTERNAL RECONNAISSANCE CAMERAS AND EQUIPMENT, FUEL TANKS OR BOTH

Cutaway view of an F-104G. Lockheed

seat ejected downward and out; (4) the pilot's automatic-opening seat belt unsnapped, freeing him from the seat; and (5) the parachute opened at a preset altitude for his safe parachute descent.

Judged adequate for medium- to high-altitude emergencies, the Lockheed-engineered downward-firing ejection seat system was worthless for low-altitude emergencies. Therefore, it was subsequently replaced by upward-firing systems albeit the first one was not employed by all F-104s.

Upward-Firing Systems

The F-104's first upward-firing emergency ejection seat system was also developed by Lockheed. Designated C-2, this system was employed in all F-104s except those built in Belgium, Germany, and the Netherlands. The latter countries employed the Martin-Baker zero-zero (zero speed, zero altitude) Mk GQ7(F) upward-firing ejection seat after 1966. Once the upward-firing seats became

standard equipment, F-104 pilots felt safer in their hot-rod Starfighters.

There were problems with the Martin-Baker seats, however. After several German pilots were killed during ejection, confidence in these seats was as low as for the downward-firing seats. A team of experts was brought in to determine the cause of the problem. They disarmed a seat, put a six-foot pilot in the seat, and then hoisted the seat up and out of the F-104's cockpit to simulate an ejection. They discovered that the pilot's knees would not clear the windshield because the seat parachute placed the pilot too far forward. The seat was subsequently modified to correct the problem, and it has worked well since.

Propulsion System

If the F-104 was to outshine any other turbojet-powered fighter plane in the world, whether in development or service, the dedicated team of Lockheed Skunk Works propulsion engineers had

to find the right engine for it. They thoroughly investigated all current and forthcoming turbojet engines. Their investigations showed that several forthcoming turbojet engines, albeit unproven, might be appropriate. These included the Allison J71, which was projected to produce up to 14,000lb thrust with afterburning; the Pratt & Whitney J75, which was projected to produce up to 21,000lb thrust with afterburning; the General Electric J79, which was projected to produce up to 15,000lb thrust with afterburning.

Lockheed selected the J79 because of its better specific fuel consumption and lighter dry weight than either the J71 or J75. Moreover, the J79 was to be available sooner than the J75, which was the early favorite due to its higher thrust. The J71 was the first to be eliminated from the selection process.

Lockheed's choice of the forthcoming General Electric J79

(designated X24A under secret project MX-2118 at the time) for the F-104's propulsion system was frozen in early 1953. However, the J79 was not scheduled to be available until early 1956. To meet contractor Phase I flight-test requirements—to begin in early 1954—Lockheed was forced to find a suitable interim turbojet engine.

Following another careful selection process, Lockheed's Skunk Works propulsion engineers settled on the Wright Aeronautical J65—an Americanized version of the British Armstrong-Siddeley Sapphire—being license-built in the US by Wright and the Buick Motor Division of the General Motors Corporation. The J65 Sapphire, in various forms, was advertised to produce up to 7,800lb military thrust and 10,300lb maximum thrust (i.e., without and with afterburning).

Still, able to do nothing about it, the preferred afterburning Wright J65-W-7 would not be available for some time after the aircraft's initial flight tests were scheduled to begin. To get the first XF-104 airborne on time, Lockheed was compelled to use the nonafterburning 7,200lb thrust Buick-built J65-B-3 turbojet engine.

Oddly, since the F-104 was being designed to use two different propulsion systems, Lockheed was forced to design two different airframes—one to employ the J65 and the other to employ the J79. Moreover, each airframe needed different engine air inlets and exhaust outlets.

The decision by Lockheed to use the interim J65 proved to be a good one. Although it produced some 4,500lb less than the initial J79 (in afterburner), the afterburning Wright J65-W-7 propelled the XF-104 to Mach 1.79. Furthermore, the nonafterburning J65-B-3 powered the XF-104 to Mach 1.51. These speeds, though lower than later J79-powered F-104 speeds, were quite respectable at the time. And, even with the interim J65, test pilots knew they had a proverbial tiger by the tail.

On 8 June 1954, some three months after XF-104 number one was flying, the XJ79-GE-1 (serial number 030-001) was test-fired for the first time in a special test cell within General Electric's Evendale, Ohio, facility. Without afterburning, it produced 9,290lb thrust.

On 20 May 1955, some fourteen months after XF-104 number one was

Over-the-shoulder view of XF-104 cockpit; to-port-opening cockpit canopy is noteworthy. Lockheed

flying, the YJ79-GE-1 became airborne for the first time suspended from the bomb bay of a modified North American B-45C Tornado engine test bed. Then on 8 December 1955, the same YJ79-GE-1 engine made its first solo flight. Piloted by General Electric test pilot Roy Pryor, a General Electric-leased Douglas XF4D-1 Skyray made a successful test flight. And, following subsequent J79-powered Skyray flights, the USAF accepted the J79 as a flightworthy engine. Soon after, Lockheed began receiving production J79-GE-3s for its fleet of seventeen YF-104As. The production J79-GE-3s produced 9,300lb military thrust and 14,800lb maximum thrust. A YF-104A soon achieved doublesonic speed with this engine. On 27 April 1956, the number one YF-104A shot past Mach 2 in level flight, making the Starfighter the world's first doublesonic fighter.

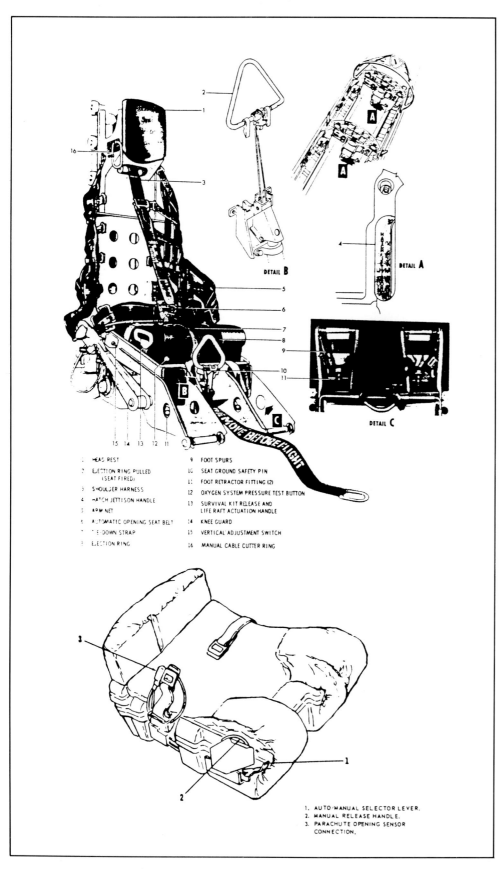

1. HEAD REST
2. EJECTION RING PULLED (SEAT FIRED)
3. SHOULDER HARNESS
4. HATCH JETTISON HANDLE
5. ARM NET
6. AUTOMATIC OPENING SEAT BELT
7. TIE DOWN STRAP
8. EJECTION RING

9. FOOT SPURS
10. SEAT GROUND SAFETY PIN
11. FOOT RETRACTOR FITTING (2)
12. OXYGEN SYSTEM PRESSURE TEST BUTTON
13. SURVIVAL KIT RELEASE AND LIFE RAFT ACTUATION HANDLE
14. KNEE GUARD
15. VERTICAL ADJUSTMENT SWITCH
16. MANUAL CABLE CUTTER RING

1. AUTO/MANUAL SELECTOR LEVER.
2. MANUAL RELEASE HANDLE.
3. PARACHUTE OPENING SENSOR CONNECTION.

Original downward-firing ejection seat and survival kit. USAF via Detail & Scale, Inc.

As different models of the F-104 developed, so did new versions of the J79. Although there are many models of the J79, F-104s used the following versions: J79-GE-3/3A with 9,300lb military thrust and 14,800lb maximum thrust; J79-GE-3B with 9,600lb military thrust and 14,800lb maximum thrust; J79-GE-7A with 10,000lb military thrust and 15,800lb maximum thrust; J79-GE-11A with 10,000lb military thrust and 15,800lb maximum thrust; J79-GE-19 with 11,870lb military thrust, 17,900lb maximum thrust.

As the J79 was refined, its thrust increased remarkably. In fact, the final version of the J79 produced more than 19,000lb maximum thrust—one-third more than the first.

As an advanced development of the axial-flow General Electric J73 (the J79 was initially designated J73-GE-X24A), the axial-flow J79 was the world's first Mach 2-rated turbojet engine and the first to feature a variable stator system to regulate airflow in the compressor section at all flight conditions and speeds. Variable stators are now the status quo.

Though it was an advanced feature, the variable stator system caused some unexpected problems that claimed the lives of several pilots at Eglin AFB. When skin sensors heated up to a threshold temperature, the system would cut off airflow to the engine to retard thrust (the system was designed to prevent the Starfighter's engine from propelling the ultra-slippery craft to speeds that would cause enough air friction to overheat the airframe). The intense sun beating down on the Eglin ramp would sometimes heatsoak the F-104 airframes beyond this threshold temperature, but their engines would develop full power on runup and on the takeoff run because the system didn't retard engine power until the aircraft's landing gear and flaps were retracted. Immediately after takeoff, the gear and flaps were retracted, with fatal results. The system would shut off airflow to the engine, the pilots would radio, "Flameout!" and the small-winged Starfighter would plummet back to earth for a fiery crash. The pilots had two choices: ride the aircraft back to the ground or be shot straight into it by the downward-firing ejection seat. Four pilots died before the cause was determined and corrected.

The J79 became a hallmark turbojet engine, powering such notable aircraft as

the General Dynamics (Convair) B-58 Hustler (for which it was originally developed), the North American A-5 Vigilante, and the McDonnell Douglas F-4 Phantom.

Armaments and Ordnance

Originally designed to carry a single 20mm cannon and a pair of guided air-to-air missiles (one on either wingtip only), the F-104 Starfighter evolved into a multi-mission fighter-interceptor, fighter-bomber, and strike fighter aircraft able to carry a wide range of armaments and ordnance for varied applications. These included the following:

General Electric M61A1 Vulcan cannon—Initially developed as a self-defense weapon for the Convair B-58

The original prototype XJ79-GE-1 turbojet engine headed for General Electric's test cell for its first firing on 8 June 1954; first test

run produced 14,350lb afterburning thrust.
General Electric

Hustler bomber, the General Electric M61A1 Vulcan, a 20mm Gatling-type (rotary-action) six-barrel cannon, was first used on the F-104 fighter. The M61A1 has a length of 73.8in and a diameter of 13.5in. It weighs 265lb with a muzzle velocity of 3,400 feet per second; its rate of fire is variable up to 6,000 rounds per minute. In the F-104, it was fed by a 20mm ammunition drum holding 725 rounds.

Ford Aerospace/Raytheon AIM-9 Sidewinder missile—The F-104 could carry up to four AIM-9 Sidewinder air-to-air missiles—two AIM-9B (radar-guided)

and two AIM-9G (heat-seeking)—one on either wingtip and two on the centerline. The Air Intercept Missile (AIM) 9 Sidewinder weighs up to 200lb and is classed as a short-range dogfighting missile. Its length is about 113in with a 5in diameter.

Selenia Aspide 1A missile—Carried by Fiat-built F-104S and Aeritalia-built F-104S ASA Starfighters only (one under either wing), this AIM-7E Sparrow derivative is produced by Selenia of Italy and is classed as a medium- to long-range air-to-air missile. The Selenia Aspide 1A

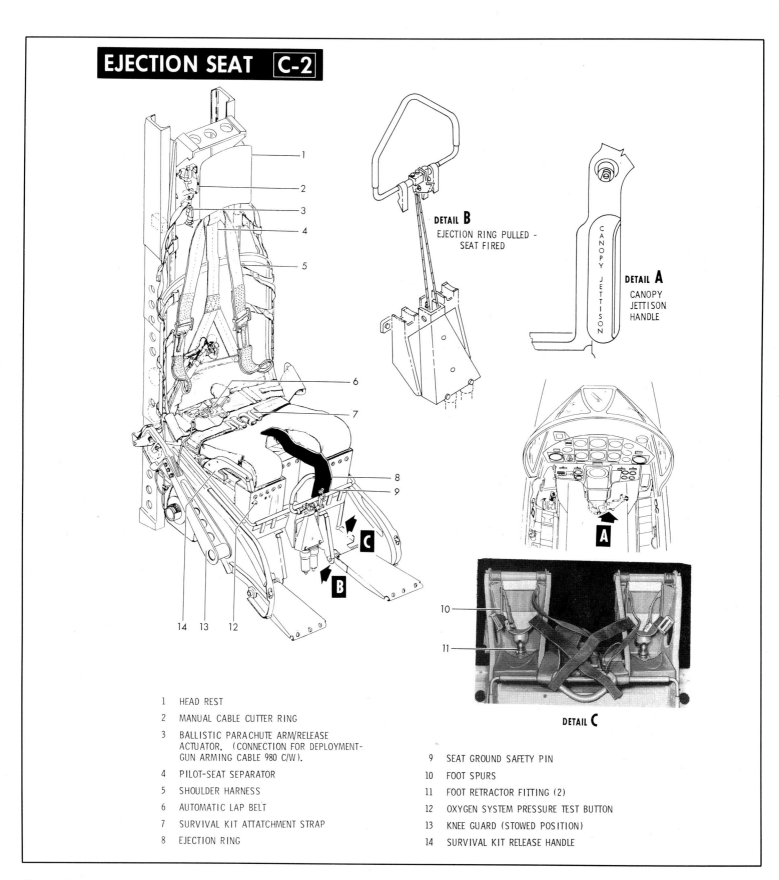

EJECTION SEAT C-2

DETAIL B
EJECTION RING PULLED –
SEAT FIRED

DETAIL A
CANOPY
JETTISON
HANDLE

CANOPY JETTISON

DETAIL C

1	HEAD REST
2	MANUAL CABLE CUTTER RING
3	BALLISTIC PARACHUTE ARM/RELEASE ACTUATOR. (CONNECTION FOR DEPLOYMENT-GUN ARMING CABLE 980 C/W).
4	PILOT-SEAT SEPARATOR
5	SHOULDER HARNESS
6	AUTOMATIC LAP BELT
7	SURVIVAL KIT ATTATCHMENT STRAP
8	EJECTION RING
9	SEAT GROUND SAFETY PIN
10	FOOT SPURS
11	FOOT RETRACTOR FITTING (2)
12	OXYGEN SYSTEM PRESSURE TEST BUTTON
13	KNEE GUARD (STOWED POSITION)
14	SURVIVAL KIT RELEASE HANDLE

*The Air Force manual drawing of the
Lockheed-designed upward-firing ejection
seat.* USAF via James C. Goodall

S/R-2 EJECTION SEAT

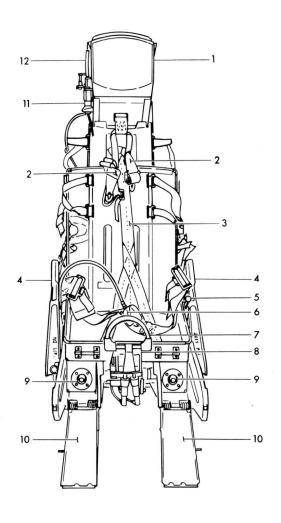
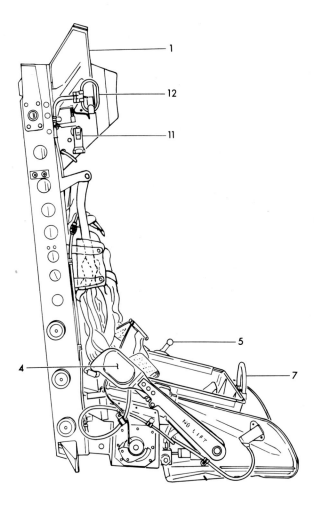

1	HEADREST	7	EJECTION RING
2	SHOULDER HARNESS	8	EJECTION RING SAFETY PIN
3	PILOT SEAT SEPARATOR	9	FOOT RETAINER BALL ASSEMBLY
4	KNEE GUARD	10	FOOT RAMP
5	INERTIA REEL LOCK HANDLE	11	DEPLOYMENT-GUN ARMING CABLE CONNECTOR
6	AUTOMATIC LAP-BELT (HBU-4/A)	12	MANUAL FOOT-CABLE CUTTER RING

The Air Force manual drawing of the improved S/R-2 ejection seat. This seat *offered true zero-speed, zero-altitude capability.* USAF via James C. Goodall

TYPICAL INSTRUMENT PANEL [A] FORWARD COCKPIT [B]

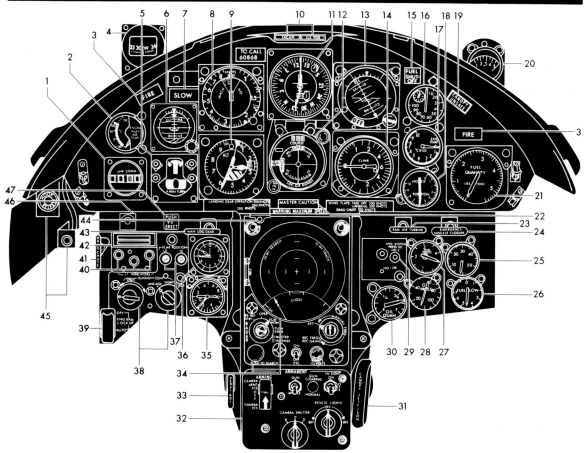

1	REMOTE CHANNEL FREQUENCY INDICATOR	
2	COMPRESSOR INLET TEMPERATURE GAGE	
3	FIRE WARNING LIGHTS (2)	
4	STANDBY COMPASS	
5	TURN-AND-SLIP INDICATOR	
6	STANDBY ATTITUDE INDICATOR	
7	COMPRESSOR INLET TEMPERATURE WARNING LIGHT	
8	AIRSPEED AND MACH NUMBER INDICATOR	
9	ALTIMETER	
10	TACAN-ILS/VOR INDICATOR LIGHTS	
11	BEARING DISTANCE HEADING INDICATOR (ID-526)	
12	COURSE INDICATOR	
13	ATTITUDE INDICATOR	
14	VERTICAL VELOCITY INDICATOR	
15	MAIN FUEL SHUTOFF VALVE WARNING LIGHT	
16	TACHOMETER	
17	EXHAUST GAS TEMPERATURE GAGE	
18	EXHAUST NOZZLE POSITION INDICATOR	
19	CANOPY UNSAFE (FLASHING) WARNING LIGHT	
20	AUTOMATIC PITCH CONTROL INDICATOR	
21	FUEL QUANTITY INDICATOR	
22	MASTER CAUTION LIGHT AND RESET BAR	
23	RAM AIR TURBINE EXTENSION HANDLE	
■24	EMERGENCY NOZZLE CLOSURE HANDLE [19] [11A] [11B]	
25	CABIN ALTIMETER	

26	FUEL FLOW INDICATOR
27	HYDRAULIC SYSTEMS PRESSURE GAGE
28	OIL PRESSURE GAGE
29	HYDRAULIC SYSTEMS PRESSURE GAGE SELECTOR SWITCH
30	NUCLEONIC OIL QUANTITY INDICATOR
31	CANOPY JETTISON HANDLE
32	ARMAMENT CONTROL PANEL [A]
33	RUDDER PEDAL ADJUSTMENT HANDLE
34	RADAR INDICATOR AND CONTROL PANEL
35	ACCELEROMETER
36	CLOCK
37	WING FLAP POSITION INDICATORS
38	GUNSIGHT CONTROL SWITCHES
39	INLET GUIDE VANES SWITCH [3B] RPM LOCKUP OVERRIDE SWITCH [19]
40	LANDING GEAR POSITION INDICATOR LIGHTS
41	DRAG CHUTE HANDLE
42	STABILIZER AND AILERON TAKEOFF TRIM INDICATOR LIGHTS
43	MANUAL LANDING GEAR RELEASE HANDLE
44	FLAP ASYMMETRY WARNING LIGHT
45	ARRESTING HOOK RELEASE BUTTON AND ARRESTING HOOK DOWN WARNING LIGHT
46	RADAR LOCK-ON SENSITIVITY CONTROL
47	VG1 PUSH-TO-ERECT

The Air Force manual drawing of the F-104A instrument panel. USAF via James C. Goodall

TYPICAL AFT COCKPIT-INSTRUMENT PANEL B

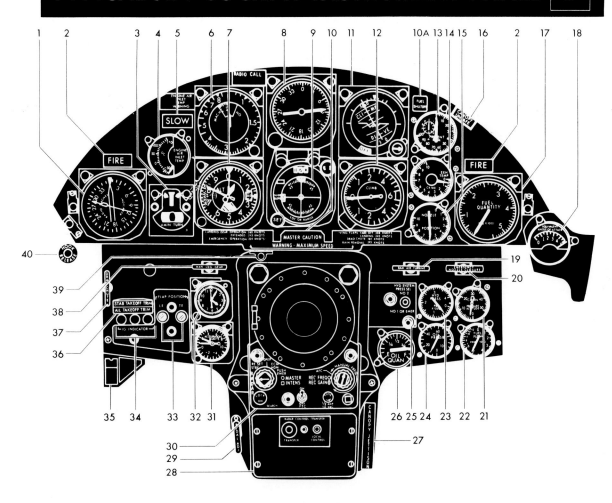

1	RADIO MAGNETIC INDICATOR
2	FIRE WARNING LIGHT (2)
3	TURN-AND-SLIP INDICATOR
4	COMPRESSOR INLET TEMPERATURE GAGE
5	COMPRESSOR INLET TEMPERATURE WARNING LIGHT
6	AIRSPEED AND MACH NUMBER INDICATOR
7	ALTIMETER
8	HEADING INDICATOR
9	COURSE INDICATOR
10	MASTER CAUTION LIGHT AND RESET BAR
10A	MAIN FUEL SHUTOFF VALVE WARNING LIGHT
11	ATTITUDE INDICATOR
12	VERTICAL VELOCITY INDICATOR
13	TACHOMETER
14	EXHAUST GAS TEMPERATURE GAGE
15	EXHAUST NOZZLE POSITION INDICATOR
16	CANOPY UNSAFE (FLASHING) WARNING LIGHT
17	FUEL QUANTITY INDICATOR
18	AUTOMATIC PITCH CONTROL INDICATOR
19	RAM AIR TURBINE EXTENSION HANDLE
■ 20	EMERGENCY NOZZLE CLOSURE HANDLE 19 11A 11B

21	CABIN ALTIMETER
22	FUEL FLOW INDICATOR
23	HYDRAULIC SYSTEMS PRESSURE INDICATOR
24	OIL PRESSURE GAGE
25	HYDRAULIC SYSTEMS PRESSURE SELECTOR SWITCH
26	NUCLEONIC OIL QUANTITY INDICATOR
27	CANOPY JETTISON HANDLE
28	RADAR CONTROL TRANSFER PANEL
29	RUDDER PEDAL ADJUSTMENT HANDLE
30	RADAR INDICATOR AND CONTROL PANEL
31	ACCELEROMETER
32	CLOCK
33	WING FLAP POSITION INDICATORS
34	LANDING GEAR POSITION INDICATOR LIGHTS
35	INLET GUIDE VANES SWITCH 3B RPM LOCKUP OVERRIDE SWITCH 19
36	STABILIZER AND AILERON TAKEOFF TRIM INDICATOR LIGHTS
37	DRAG CHUTE HANDLE
38	MANUAL LANDING GEAR RELEASE HANDLE
39	FLAP ASYMMETRY WARNING LIGHT
40	ARRESTING HOOK RELEASE BUTTON

*The Air Force manual drawing of the
F-104B's rear-cockpit instrument panel.*
USAF via James C. Goodall

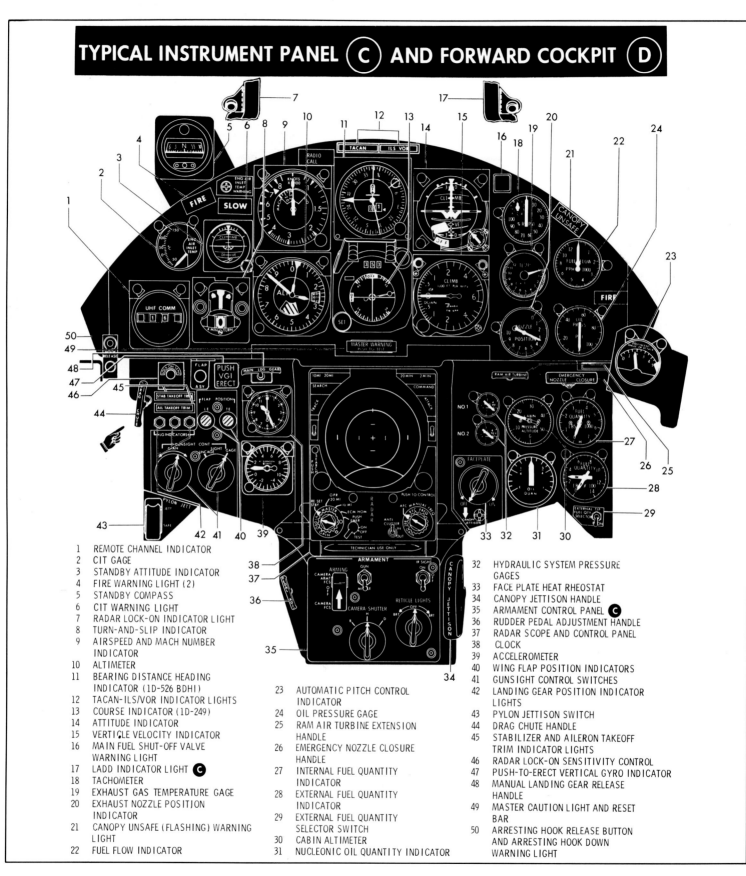

TYPICAL INSTRUMENT PANEL Ⓒ AND FORWARD COCKPIT Ⓓ

1 REMOTE CHANNEL INDICATOR
2 CIT GAGE
3 STANDBY ATTITUDE INDICATOR
4 FIRE WARNING LIGHT (2)
5 STANDBY COMPASS
6 CIT WARNING LIGHT
7 RADAR LOCK-ON INDICATOR LIGHT
8 TURN-AND-SLIP INDICATOR
9 AIRSPEED AND MACH NUMBER
   INDICATOR
10 ALTIMETER
11 BEARING DISTANCE HEADING
   INDICATOR (1D-526 BDHI)
12 TACAN-ILS/VOR INDICATOR LIGHTS
13 COURSE INDICATOR (1D-249)
14 ATTITUDE INDICATOR
15 VERTICLE VELOCITY INDICATOR
16 MAIN FUEL SHUT-OFF VALVE
   WARNING LIGHT
17 LADD INDICATOR LIGHT Ⓒ
18 TACHOMETER
19 EXHAUST GAS TEMPERATURE GAGE
20 EXHAUST NOZZLE POSITION
   INDICATOR
21 CANOPY UNSAFE (FLASHING) WARNING
   LIGHT
22 FUEL FLOW INDICATOR

23 AUTOMATIC PITCH CONTROL
   INDICATOR
24 OIL PRESSURE GAGE
25 RAM AIR TURBINE EXTENSION
   HANDLE
26 EMERGENCY NOZZLE CLOSURE
   HANDLE
27 INTERNAL FUEL QUANTITY
   INDICATOR
28 EXTERNAL FUEL QUANTITY
   INDICATOR
29 EXTERNAL FUEL QUANTITY
   SELECTOR SWITCH
30 CABIN ALTIMETER
31 NUCLEONIC OIL QUANTITY INDICATOR

32 HYDRAULIC SYSTEM PRESSURE
   GAGES
33 FACE PLATE HEAT RHEOSTAT
34 CANOPY JETTISON HANDLE
35 ARMAMENT CONTROL PANEL Ⓒ
36 RUDDER PEDAL ADJUSTMENT HANDLE
37 RADAR SCOPE AND CONTROL PANEL
38 CLOCK
39 ACCELEROMETER
40 WING FLAP POSITION INDICATORS
41 GUNSIGHT CONTROL SWITCHES
42 LANDING GEAR POSITION INDICATOR
   LIGHTS
43 PYLON JETTISON SWITCH
44 DRAG CHUTE HANDLE
45 STABILIZER AND AILERON TAKEOFF
   TRIM INDICATOR LIGHTS
46 RADAR LOCK-ON SENSITIVITY CONTROL
47 PUSH-TO-ERECT VERTICAL GYRO INDICATOR
48 MANUAL LANDING GEAR RELEASE
   HANDLE
49 MASTER CAUTION LIGHT AND RESET
   BAR
50 ARRESTING HOOK RELEASE BUTTON
   AND ARRESTING HOOK DOWN
   WARNING LIGHT

The Air Force manual drawing of the instrument panel in the F-104C and in the F-104D's front cockpit. USAF via James C. Goodall

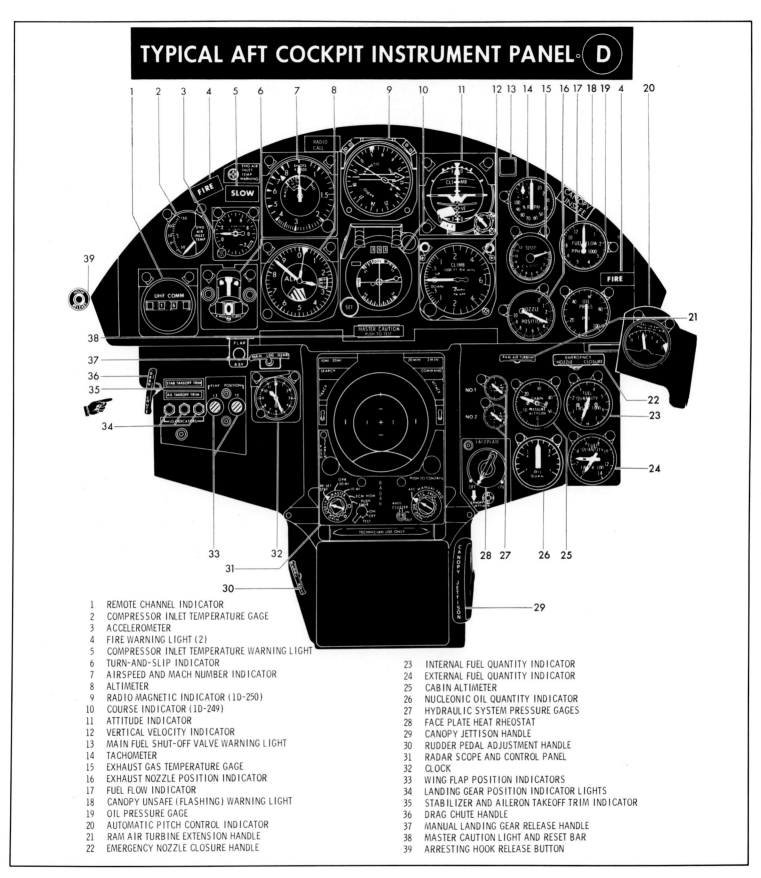

TYPICAL AFT COCKPIT INSTRUMENT PANEL · D

1	REMOTE CHANNEL INDICATOR	
2	COMPRESSOR INLET TEMPERATURE GAGE	
3	ACCELEROMETER	
4	FIRE WARNING LIGHT (2)	
5	COMPRESSOR INLET TEMPERATURE WARNING LIGHT	
6	TURN-AND-SLIP INDICATOR	
7	AIRSPEED AND MACH NUMBER INDICATOR	
8	ALTIMETER	
9	RADIO MAGNETIC INDICATOR (1D-250)	
10	COURSE INDICATOR (1D-249)	
11	ATTITUDE INDICATOR	
12	VERTICAL VELOCITY INDICATOR	
13	MAIN FUEL SHUT-OFF VALVE WARNING LIGHT	
14	TACHOMETER	
15	EXHAUST GAS TEMPERATURE GAGE	
16	EXHAUST NOZZLE POSITION INDICATOR	
17	FUEL FLOW INDICATOR	
18	CANOPY UNSAFE (FLASHING) WARNING LIGHT	
19	OIL PRESSURE GAGE	
20	AUTOMATIC PITCH CONTROL INDICATOR	
21	RAM AIR TURBINE EXTENSION HANDLE	
22	EMERGENCY NOZZLE CLOSURE HANDLE	

23	INTERNAL FUEL QUANTITY INDICATOR
24	EXTERNAL FUEL QUANTITY INDICATOR
25	CABIN ALTIMETER
26	NUCLEONIC OIL QUANTITY INDICATOR
27	HYDRAULIC SYSTEM PRESSURE GAGES
28	FACE PLATE HEAT RHEOSTAT
29	CANOPY JETTISON HANDLE
30	RUDDER PEDAL ADJUSTMENT HANDLE
31	RADAR SCOPE AND CONTROL PANEL
32	CLOCK
33	WING FLAP POSITION INDICATORS
34	LANDING GEAR POSITION INDICATOR LIGHTS
35	STABILIZER AND AILERON TAKEOFF TRIM INDICATOR
36	DRAG CHUTE HANDLE
37	MANUAL LANDING GEAR RELEASE HANDLE
38	MASTER CAUTION LIGHT AND RESET BAR
39	ARRESTING HOOK RELEASE BUTTON

The Air Force manual drawing of the
F-104D's rear-cockpit instrument panel.
USAF via James C. Goodall

weighs about 500lb with a 145in length and 8in diameter. Its guidance is by a Selenia monopulse semi-active radar homing system. Under a license agreement with Raytheon, development of this missile by Selenia began in 1969. The missile entered service in 1979.

Fire control systems—The F-104 used four different radar-directed fire control systems: the AN/ASG-14T-1 and AN/ASG-14T-2, F15A North American Search and Ranging Radar system (NASARR), and R21G/M1. Three were US developed and produced, and the fourth was developed and produced by Italy.

External fuel tanks—The F-104 was designed to carry a number of auxiliary, jettisonable external fuel tanks to extend its range. Variously, these tanks hold 170 (wingtip), 195 (underwing pylon) and 225 (underfuselage pylon) gallons; total amount of external fuel that could be carried was 955 gallons.

Conventional weapons—The F-104 could carry up to three 1,000lb Mk 117, three 750lb Mk 83, three 500lb Mk 82, or two 2,000lb Mk 84 free-fall conventional bombs.

Nuclear weapons—The F-104 could carry two types of nuclear weapons—a single Mk 28 nuclear bomb or a single McDonnell Douglas AIR-2 Genie air-to-air nuclear missile. The Mk 28 was carried ventrally on centerline, while the Genie was carried the same way but on a retractable, trapeze-like launcher.

Optional Ordnance—As with most tactical fighter aircraft, the F-104 could carry just about any armaments and ordnance produced during its day.

The original service test YJ79-GE-1 was first flight-tested under power beneath a modified North American B-45C Tornado bomber.
Rockwell International

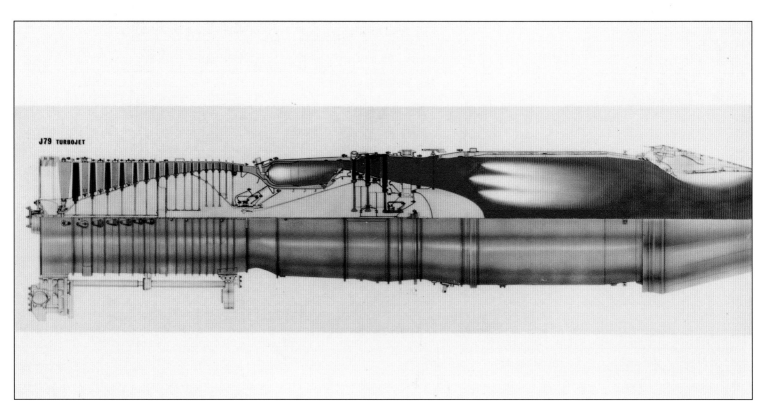

*Cutaway of J79 turbojet engine illustrates
afterburning mode.* General Electric

A production J79-GE-7A turbojet engine.
General Electric

Chapter 7

Foreign Starfighters

Because its priorities had changed, the USAF did not procure any additional Starfighters for either Air Defense Command or Tactical Air Command after fiscal year 1957. Not counting procurement of two prototype XF-104s, follow-on contracts brought the final USAF total to 294 Starfighters (247 single-seat F-104A/Cs, forty-seven tandem-seat F-104B/Ds). Still, worldwide interest in the Starfighter remained high, and Lockheed set its sights on selling its popular F-104 to as many foreign air forces as possible.

To do this, however, Lockheed had to first defeat strong contenders from several other American airframe contractors, including the Grumman F11F-1F Super Tiger, North American F-100J Super Sabre, and the Northrop Model N-156F (later F-5A) Freedom

The Grumman F11F-1F Super Tiger was Lockheed's closest rival for fighter sales to foreign governments. Grumman

The proposed North American F-100J Super Sabre was never built. Rockwell International

Fighter. At the time, only the Grumman F11F-1F Super Tiger—a General Electric J79-powered version of its Wright J65-powered F-11A Tiger (formerly F11F-1)—was actually flying. The North American F-100J Super Sabre and the Northrop Model N-156F Freedom Fighter were paper proposals.

Grumman had built two F11F-1F Super Tiger demonstrators in hope of selling the type to the US Navy and foreign users. The Super Tiger, like the

Starfighter, generated a great deal of interest from abroad, so a fly-off competition—on paper and in the air—was scheduled.

After experienced fighter pilots from the Luftwaffe flew the F11F-1F and the F-104C, the Starfighter prevailed. Since no orders for the F11F-1F were forthcoming, it became a footnote in aviation history. The Super Tiger demonstrated exceptional performance, but the Starfighter won because it was better.

The F-104G

On 6 November 1958, the German Federal Republic's Defense Committee selected the Starfighter to serve as their nation's primary fighter-interceptor, fighter-bomber, and photographic reconnaissance aircraft. Procurement contracts were signed with West Germany on 18 March 1959. The initial order called for thirty two-seat F-104F trainers and sixty-six advanced single-seat, multi-mission F-104G (G for

If it had been flying, the Northrop Model N-156F Freedom Fighter might have given the F-104 a run for its money; this is the full- *scale engineering mockup of the N-156F (later F-5A).* Northrop

Germany) fighter aircraft. Deliveries began in late 1959 from the production lines in Burbank, California, until production could begin under license in Europe. Lockheed produced all thirty F-104Fs and ninety-six F-104Gs (thirty more than the original F-104G order) before production began in Europe.

Lockheed made a number of design changes in the F-104 to adapt it as the F-104G fighter-bomber. The Starfighter's fuselage, wing, and empennage were strengthened so the aircraft could carry an increased payload. Adequate strength for the air-to-ground role with heavy

ordnance caused some increase in gross weight—about 1,000lb. Yet, only 350lb were added to the airframe. The remaining weight increase was the result of the improved avionic systems. This new multi-mission capability was achieved with negligible performance penalty because the F-104 had been designed from the outset as an air superiority fighter, with excess power and maneuverability.

Other important changes included all-weather capability through improved avionics, the Lockheed-engineered C-2 upward-firing emergency ejection seat

system for safer exits at low altitudes, all-new avionics and fire control system; and a lightweight, fully automatic, self-contained inertial navigation system.

The F-104G was developed with all required stores stations and weapons controls for intercept, strike, and close support missions. The aircraft's weapons system was designed so it could be configured to the required mission profile by carrying more fuel and fewer bombs and missiles, or vice versa.

Using the F-104G as a model, Lockheed announced they could offer a new international version to meet any air

An early production F-104G destined for duty in the Luftwaffe. Lockheed

This tandem-seat TF-104G (Free World Defender) was retained by Lockheed for a time to demonstrate the type to potential customers abroad. While still in Lockheed's hands, it was flown to Mach 2-plus at 35,000ft and cross-country by Toni LeVier, and it was used by the late Jacqueline Cochran for her trio of world speed records for women; it later went to the Dutch air force. Lockheed

A Royal Canadian Air Force CF-104.
Lockheed

force needs, and a succession of orders followed.

To start, Lockheed finalized a license agreement with Canadair on 24 July 1959 to provide 200 CF-104s for eight Royal Canadian Air Force squadrons serving with NATO forces in Europe.

The Netherlands completed a licensing agreement on 20 April 1960 for F-104Gs. On 20 June, Belgium signed a similar agreement.

Japan announced plans in November 1960 to equip its new Japan Air Self-Defense Force with the F-104J, to serve strictly as an air superiority fighter. A Japanese industrial team headed by Mitsubishi Heavy Industries, including Kawasaki Aircraft, Limited, was given responsibility by the Japanese government for the production of 210 F-104Js.

On 2 March 1961, Italy announced it would join Belgium, West Germany, and the Netherlands in a production program to build F-104 Starfighters, which had suddenly become the free world's premier fighter aircraft.

By 1 September 1962, F-104s were being built in seven countries on three continents. Starfighters manufactured or assembled in Germany, Belgium, Italy, and the Netherlands (along with those coproduced in the US) were the backbone of NATO's aerial defense in Europe. The use of identical master tooling by all manufacturers ensured complete interchangeability of parts and assemblies between countries. In effect, a part made in one country would fit an assembly made in any other country.

These aircraft were designed around the G configuration. Their tremendous power reserve, especially with afterburning, gave them unmatched performance among fighters of the world. For example, within twenty seconds after brake release, an F-104G would be airborne and flying at a speed of 525mph.

A Japanese Air Self-Defense Force F-104J.
Lockheed

Seconds later, it would reach Mach 0.90. Climbing at an angle of thirty-five degrees, it would reach 40,000ft in just one minute and forty seconds. In another thirty-five seconds, it would be at 50,000ft.

By this time, the F-104 program had become the largest integrated weapon system development and production program ever undertaken by a group of free-world nations. The program represented a great step forward for the European aerospace industry in the development of advanced aircraft weapon systems. It provided the medium that permitted NATO nations to work together in cooperative fashion toward common goals. Undoubtedly, it established a pattern for future programs such as the eighteen-nation participation in the General Dynamics F-16 multi-national fighter program.

European production sites were concentrated according to geographical groupings of leading aircraft companies. The South Group (Arbeitsgemeinschaft Sud) included Dornier, Heinkel, Messerschmitt (later Messerschmitt-Bolkow-Blohm [MBB]), and Siebel. This group built 210 single-seat F-104s. Final assembly and the flight-test phases were conducted at Manching, Germany.

The North Group (Arge Nord) formed when the Netherlands chose the F-104. It included two Netherlands companies—Fokker and Aviolanda—and three German companies—Focke-Wulf, Hamburger Flugzeugbau, and Weserflugzeugbau. The total workload in the production of 350 Starfighter aircraft was evenly divided in both countries.

The West Group was a combination of SABCA (Societe Anonyme de Constructions Aeronautiques) and Avions Fairey S.A. in Belgium, joined by Fiat and

A fine study of an F-104J. Lockheed

other Italian firms in production of 188 F-104G aircraft for Belgium and Germany. Fiat's Turin facility was the site of additional final work and flight evaluation of another 200 F-104Gs for Italy.

At first, all production of two-seat F-104s was performed by Lockheed-California at its Burbank and Palmdale facilities. Then in 1964, after licensees in Germany has phased out their production of single-seat aircraft, Lockheed initiated a coproduction program with four foreign airframe contractors to produce thirty-two two-seat Starfighters.

Under a unique arrangement to minimize tooling costs and provide additional production in Germany, Lockheed made detailed parts and assemblies that were peculiar to the two-seat F-104s. Meanwhile, foreign manufacturers made parts and assemblies that were common to both single- and two-seat F-104s.

A follow-on program in 1965 resulted in production of forty-six two-seat TF-104Gs for Germany, the Netherlands, and Belgium. All but ten of these were assembled in Europe.

One of the best indicators of the rapid production buildup can be shown by the first delivery dates of foreign-built aircraft to operational units: Canada's CF-104, March 1961; Germany's F-104G, March 1962; the Netherlands' F-104G, April 1962; Belgium's F-104G, June 1962; Japan's F-104J, September 1962; and Italy's F-104G, September 1962.

In 1962 the US Air Force ordered 140 F-104Gs from Canada for various NATO nations under the Military Assistance

A Luftwaffe F-104G with a pair of AIM-9 Sidewinder missiles. Lockheed

Toni LeVier in the front cockpit of Lockheed's TF-104G ready for takeoff on her flight to Mach 2 at 35,000ft. She flew the entire flight from just after takeoff to just before landing. Lockheed

My Incredible Flights
by Toni LeVier

Born on 21 September 1944 in Glendale, California, Toni LeVier was taught to fly by Sammy Mason in a Beechcraft Musketeer at the age of eighteen, and with a total of only forty solo hours, she enrolled in her father's F-104 flight school. There, she received a Class I medical examination, pressure chamber tests to 40,000ft, and F-104 pilot training in both normal and emergency procedures. This was followed by her flight to Mach 2 at 35,000ft with full afterburning thrust in a tandem seat F-104 Starfighter to become the world's fastest schoolgirl while her father, Tony LeVier, sat in the rear cockpit and enjoyed the ride. Toni LeVier, at the time, was the living mascot of the 479th TFW at George AFB, California. She currently resides in Aptos, California, with husband Richard and son Bryan.

The morning of 31 May 1963 was very still at Palmdale Airport, California. I could already feel the sultry breeze indicating it was going to be another hot day in the Mojave Desert. The early morning sky had a pinkish grey cast to it, and I could feel a repeat anxiousness come over me.

I had already had a most memorable experience two days earlier, going Mach 2 in the company-owned Lockheed F-104 *Free World Defender* (a tandem seat TF-104G Starfighter my dad's employer used as a demonstrator aircraft for potential customers), with myself in the front cockpit and my father in the rear cockpit. I remember the excitement and anticipation that morning as my first flight approached; the press interviews, the picture taking, and the ground crew preparing our plane for my flight to twice the speed of sound. The ground-pounding thunder and deafening whine of the turbojet engine sent currents of excitement through my entire body. It was an experience that had always been a wishful dream to me since childhood, that of flying in a jet airplane. I remember listening to my dad in fascination as he recounted one of his memorable flights to us but always trying to avoid the more dangerous parts of them for my mother's sake, since she had a fear of flying.

As we taxied to the runway we were assigned, I began thinking of all the training I'd had leading up to this moment; would I perform as I had been taught or shrivel up and forget everything that was to be the greatest experience of my life? My father jogged me back to reality with his reassuring voice, "Toni, you might as well follow through on the takeoff, just be relaxed and light on the controls." I responded as we took the runway and stopped for a moment while my father moved the throttle forward, then a brief moment later he said, "We're now going into afterburner." At this moment I got the first impression of what jet flying was all about. The sudden surge of acceleration pushed me up against the back of my seat as the plane seemed to leap forward at an enormous rate. For a moment I was caught in the excitement as my father explained the takeoff and the speed of 185 knots (277.5mph) for rotation. Halfway down the runway with that ever present acceleration, I couldn't contain myself and blurted out, "Dad, this is the most."

I heard dad chuckle as we became airborne and then a series of clunks as the landing gear was retracted. Next came the wing flaps which are used for taking off to give the plane more lift. Things were happening so fast I wondered how anyone could possibly keep up with them. Then suddenly, dad said, "I'm pulling it out of afterburner," at which point the plane stopped accelerating so fast. At about a thousand feet above the ground, dad instructed me to unhook the parachute lanyard which is used during takeoff and landings to provide the pilot with an almost instantaneous deployment of the parachute if the pilot must eject close to the ground. At this point, dad instructed me to fly the plane and to continue climbing as he directed me to turn to a northeast direction which took us right by Edwards AFB.

I had only flown a plane with a stick once, when I was about fifteen. Dad had taken me up in a German trainer called Bucher Jungmeister, and we did some stunts, which was a lot of fun. I learned to fly in a Beech Musketeer, which had a wheel, but I think the stick made it easier, and I had no problem holding the plane level and climbing as dad had instructed. He told me to hold 0.9 Mach number in the climb to 39,000 feet and, getting clearance from Edwards AFB, we entered the supersonic corridor. With my father's guidance, I moved the throttle full forward into afterburner and nosed the plane down slightly to level off at 35,000 feet. Once again, the acceleration shoved me against the back of my seat but not as hard as it did on the takeoff.

It was almost instantly that dad told me to keep an eye on the Mach number which is part of the airspeed indicator to see when we went supersonic. It was an exciting moment as I expected something dramatic to happen—nothing did. It was no time at all that dad said, "There it is, Toni, you're now the world's first Mach 2 kid." We had gone almost 1,500mph.

Dad then directed me to pull the throttle out of afterburner, and when I did, I got another surprise of my life as the plane slowed up so violently I felt like I was being pulled in two opposite directions as my body lunged forward. I thought I would fly right straight out of the canopy window, and I grabbed at the glare shield; I'd forgotten to lock my shoulder straps. Dad reminded me about doing it slowly to avoid the tremendous reduction of thrust coming out of afterburner, but I forgot.

When we landed there were about 100 people and newsmen awaiting us with cheers. We were interviewed, and it was on the news that night.

This journey of mine started taking form about five months previously. At the time, I was a senior in high school and taking flying lessons, having just soloed. My father approached me with a plan that several executives from Lockheed thought was a good idea. This particular jet had to be delivered back to Washington,

D.C. in early June for promotional demonstrations to the USAF, and they thought this would be a great promotion in itself, showing how easy it was to fly, and its fantastic performance. Since I shared my father's first and last name and he was the first to test this jet, the stage was set for our great journey.

My training for this extraordinary event was comprised of six weeks of ground school learning the entire cockpit and focusing on the navigational part to help my father with the flight. I also used the cockpit simulator, a device you sit in that gives you a feeling and likeness of flying the aircraft itself.

I had the opportunity to go through Lockheed's famed Skunk Works Advanced Development Projects Research Lab. I was given a complete Class I physical examination and then checked out in their high-altitude decompression chamber. It's essentially a large tank that has a door, windows, and seats in it. We sat in there without our oxygen masks on as they took us through different altitudes. They more or less pump the atmosphere out, diminishing the pressure and most importantly, the oxygen, causing a condition in people known as hypoxia. This plight causes several side effects, endangering pilots and causing accidents where investigators cannot find any apparent reason for an accident, which this quiet culprit has caused. This condition makes you very silly; your mind wanders, and your brain plays tricks on you as if you were drunk. You simply cannot react to anything.

As they took more and more pressure out of the chamber, I remember laughing for no reason at all and not being able to write a simple sentence. I could hear them telling me what to do, but I could not react in any way. The technician told me to quickly hook up my oxygen, but I only sat there and smiled. With that he rushed over to me and gave me oxygen. Having gong through this experience gave me another insight into the complexities of our environment and our vulnerability without oxygen.

I was outfitted with the very best. My head was measured for a custom helmet, and once it was finished, it was a perfect fit and comfortable. It had been specially painted for me in my favorite color, powder blue, with the plane painted on it and my name above that in a beautiful script. My bright orange flying suit was the smallest Lockheed could find. They made gold plated spurs for my boots, which had sockets at the heel that fit on a ball, joined to a cable. This enabled your feet and legs to be pulled back and tucked into position if and when you pulled the ejection loop on front of the seat between your legs.

One day as my father and I were driving up to the Rye Canyon Skunk Works, he put the question to me. What if we were in trouble and had to eject? I answered with a quick reply, "I would pull the ejection loop without hesitation." My father was relieved with my answer, hoping I would not panic if that situation ever arose.

As we readied for our flight that Friday morning, the anticipation of the unknown quietly crept over me. Only a few of my very closest friends knew of my exciting venture and they probably thought it odd that I wanted to keep it quiet. I guess underneath I figured everyone would soon find out anyway, since it was put on the news and the story was picked up all over the world. For a year after I was still receiving letters and clippings from as far away as Australia, Germany, Japan, and Egypt, to name a few. I received many letters from boys in the Air Force Academy longing to know how I was so fortunate in my opportunity to fly in the F-104, which was their ultimate dream.

Leaving Palmdale, our first stopover was Albuquerque, New Mexico. Since that area is at a high altitude and we had to clear a high mountain range to come down and land, we made a rather steep and fast descent which caused my head to feel like it was

Eighteen-year-old Toni LeVier—the world's fastest schoolgirl—posed with Lockheed's TF-104G after her Mach 2 flight on 29 May 1963. Lockheed

going to explode. The excruciating pain was almost too much to bear, and the last thing that I felt like doing was being interviewed. Taking off again, we headed for Oklahoma City and were told that we might run into some bad weather, which did not affect me, until it hit. About fifteen minutes outside of Oklahoma City the ground control started to guide us by radar. We had no visibility whatsoever; our sleek bird with its wonderful maneuverability glided through this very rough weather like nothing was happening. The ceiling over Tinker AFB was under 200 feet and the raindrops were the largest I had ever seen. Our plane started hydroplaning from the amount of water on the runway, and also fighting a crosswind my father had to delay pulling the drag chute for fear of sailing off the runway. We finally came to a stop, and I was never so glad to be on the ground. I was so weak with apprehension and tension of the landing that I felt my knees begin to buckle, and a slight nervous breakdown approaching.

As we were being interviewed inside, looking like drowned rats, I couldn't get over the ridiculous questions that were put to us, wondering what form of intelligence one must have to be a reporter. My father gave me a good piece of advice, "Grin and bear it, it soon will be all over." At that time I was very aware of the feeling I had about all the interviews. I did not feel worthy of them, nor did I like being in center stage. Being with my father through this landing ordeal gave me an inner strength that I would not have had normally. He helped me all along with his calming words
Continued on next page

Toni and Tony just before their takeoff on 31 May 1963 from Palmdale, California, to Washington, D.C. Lockheed

Onward the next day to Dayton, Ohio, we passed by Saint Louis, Missouri, and my father checked in with the airway traffic control. They were aware of our flight and asked, "Is young Toni really up there?" I answered, "Yup, I'm here!"

Landing at Wright-Patterson AFB at Dayton, we were met by the General Hap Arnold Youth Society, and while my dad was preparing for our flight to Washington, D.C., I was treated royally by kids my own age. It was a memorable occasion.

We were about to take the runway when my father said, "Toni, want to make the takeoff?" I said, "Sure" and away we went. I was amazed at how easy it was. I had no trouble at all holding the aircraft straight, and when we reached 185 knots, dad said to pull the stick back to raise the nose and take off. It worked just fine and then dad took over to get us on our way.

From Dayton, Ohio, to Andrews AFB in Washington, D.C., took us only forty-five minutes at cruising speed. On our initial approach at 1,500 feet a twin-engine Cessna 310 loomed out of nowhere, zooming right across our flight path. We missed it by mere feet, and we were both shaken as never before at the impending disaster that could have taken place. We tried to get him traced, but to no avail. Everyone was bewildered by the fact that a civilian plane was in our airspace, which is restricted and against the law for civilian aircraft.

We finally landed with a large and happy reception awaiting us. I was thrilled to be down safe, but sad my incredible flights were behind me. What made this fantastic experience so special to me was not just the experience itself, but that my father and I did it together.

and understanding in his confident, humble manner. Later he told me of his slight apprehension, and we both had a good laugh, knowing it was behind us.

Program (MAP). Canadair, Limited was selected to produce the aircraft along with 200 CF-104s for the Royal Canadian Air Force. Major suppliers of equipment and accessories included DeHavilland Aircraft of Canada; United Aircraft of Canada; Canadian Westinghouse, Limited; Canadian General Electric, Limited; Canadian Aviation Electric, Limited; and Computer Devices of Canada. These MAP aircraft were in addition to the 109 aircraft—which had been produced by Lockheed in Burbank, California—previously authorized by the USAF. The first MAP F-104G was initially flight-tested on 30 July 1963. Deliveries to Denmark, Greece, Norway, Pakistan, Spain, Taiwan, and Turkey began before the end of 1963.

The worldwide production program for the F-104 moved forward at such a high rate that by 1 October 1964, more than 2,000 Starfighters bore the insignia of fourteen free-world air forces. After that time, Lockheed engineers in Burbank continued their efforts to improve the F-104.

The F-104S Super Starfighter

Lockheed modified two Italian F-104Gs for use as F-104S prototypes—essentially, to create what was dubbed the Super Starfighter. The first F-104S prototype, powered by the 17,900lb afterburning thrust General Electric J79-GE-19 turbojet, and featuring aerodynamic improvements, was initially flight-tested in December 1966. The second F-104S prototype, fitted with new avionic systems, made its first flight in March 1967.

Fiat went on to produce 164 F-104S Starfighters for the Italian air force—the first production example flying on 30 December 1968. With its new higher-thrust J79-GE-19 turbojet, the S version featured vastly improved acceleration, rate of climb, and maneuverability at all speeds and altitudes. The lower specific fuel consumption of its -19 engine allowed for increased range. The F-104S's primary role is all-weather interceptor. However, by design, the aircraft doubles as an all-weather fighter-bomber.

Fiat produced another eighty-one F-104Ss for the Turkish air force, bringing the total number of new-build F-104Ss to 245; deliveries ended in March 1979.

In December 1984, flight trials of an advanced version of the F-104S began. This version of the Starfighter, the F-104S ASA (Aggiornamento Sistema d'Arma, or updated weapon system), now featured the Fiat R21G/M1 look-down, shoot-down radar and fire control system, modern electronic countermeasures (ECM) equipment, and the ability to carry and fire the Selenia Aspide 1A medium- to long-range, radar-guided air-to-air missile based on the Raytheon AIM-7E Sparrow air-to-air missile. As the result, Italian air force units are now using F-104S ASAs—until at least 1995—that were created from former F-104Ss. The F-104S ASA has the distinction of being the last version of the Lockheed F-104 Starfighter employed by a foreign user.

In all, foreign airframe contractors produced 1,789 F-104s: Canadair built 340; Fiat built 444; Fokker built 350; Messerschmitt built 210; MBB built fifty; Mitsubishi built 207; and SABCA built 188. Moreover, Lockheed coproduced forty-eight F-104s for friendly air forces. This

A TDN CL-981 for Germany displays its load-carrying capability—nine attachment points. Lockheed

Next page
An Italian Air Force F-104S with a pair of Aspide 1A missiles. Lockheed

An Italian Air Force F-104S departs terra firma with its maximum load. Lockheed

brings the total to 1,837 Starfighters built for foreign air forces. In other words, foreign air forces received about seventy-eight percent of all F-104s built. Moreover, Germany produced more than thirty-five percent of all the Starfighters built, more F-104s than any other country—including the US.

The following section is a rundown of Lockheed F-104 Starfighter variants employed by foreign users.

A Greek F-104G. Lockheed

A Luftwaffe F-104G rolls in for a cannon-firing pass. Lockheed via Campbell Archives

F-104A: At least sixty-eight F-104As ended up in the hands of foreign air forces. One F-104A-15 (serial number 56-770) was transferred to the Royal Canadian Air Force (Canadian serial number 12700) for use as a model aircraft for the Canadian version of the Starfighter. Some twenty-five F-104As went to Taiwan, thirty-two wound up in Jordan, and ten went to Pakistan.

F-104B: There were twenty-six F-104Bs manufactured and some of them were transferred to Jordan and Taiwan after their USAF retirement, although the exact number remains unclear.

F-104DJ: Japan's Air Self-Defense Force procured twenty Lockheed-built (reassembled in Japan by Mitsubishi) F-104DJ two-seat trainer aircraft powered by the license-built J79-IHI-11A turbojet engine of 15,800lb afterburning thrust. These aircraft were basically TF-104Gs with Japanese markings. This version of the Starfighter was similar in many ways to Japan's single-seat F-104J, to be discussed later in the text. The JASDF accepted its twenty F-104DJs during July 1962 and January 1964.

F-104F: Lockheed built thirty two-seat F-104F trainers for the Luftwaffe, the F-104F being a minimum-change derivative of the USAF F-104D. The F-104Fs served with the Luftwaffe from October 1959, the date of first delivery, to December 1971 when they retired from German service. These were the first F-104s to be employed by Germany, and in the end, carried the serial numbers 2901 through 2930 (earlier BB360 through BB389). When first delivered, they carried USAF serial numbers 59-4994 through 59-5023.

F-104G: All in all, 1,122 F-104Gs were built: 139 by Lockheed, 140 by Canadair, 164 by Fiat, 231 by Fokker, fifty by MBB,

A Dutch air force F-104G. Lockheed

Previous page
A Norwegian air force F-104G. Lockheed

The first RF-104G photographic
reconnaissance plane. Lockheed

210 by Messerschmitt, and 188 by SABCA. In fact, the F-104G accounted for almost fifty percent of all F-104s built. They were built in the US by Lockheed, in Canada by Canadair, and in Europe by four main contractor groups.

Respectively, Europe's four groups' F-104G Starfighters first flew on 5 October 1960, 3 August 1961, 11 November 1961, and 9 June 1962. These four groups manufactured 210, 188, 231, and 169 F-104Gs respectively. MBB produced another fifty for the Luftwaffe in 1971–73 to replace F-104Gs lost in crashes.

F-104Gs were also used by Germany's Bundesmarine (German navy).

The first F-104G was a Lockheed-built plane based on the F-104C model but with a number of improvements. These included:

• Incorporation of the Lockheed C-2 upward-firing ejection seat, later replaced with the Martin-Baker Mk GQ7(F) zero-zero upward-firing ejection seat, beginning in 1967

• Adoption of the Autonetics F15A NASARR radar and fire control system, replacing the AN/ASG-14T-2 system
• Improved engine reliability and power with the General Electric J79-GE-11A turbojet. (European-built F-104Gs were powered by the J79-MTU-J1K turbojet license-built in Germany by MAN-Turbo.)
• Strengthened airframe to carry heavier weapons load
• Enlarged vertical fin area with fully powered rudder, similar to the two-seat versions
• Wing leading-edge combat maneuvering flaps
• Improved avionics

The Lockheed F-104G made its first flight on 7 June 1960. It was subsequently tested extensively at Edwards AFB by the USAF.

F-104G ZELL: Under German Air Force contract, at least one Luftwaffe F-104G (DA102) was modified for a series of zero-length launch (ZELL) tests in 1963 at Edwards AFB. Lockheed test pilot Ed Brown was project pilot on the program.

Trailer-mounted, this F-104G was able to blast off (not take off) without a runway. To do this, it relied on its J79 turbojet engine (running at either military or afterburning thrust) and its 130,000lb thrust Rocketdyne booster rocket. In a mere four seconds after blast-off, the booster dropped off and the F-104G would be flying at 280mph. The program was classified and was not disclosed to the public until 21 March 1966. Of his first ZELL takeoff, former US Navy pilot Ed Brown said:

It was one of the easiest takeoffs I ever made. All I did was push the rocket booster button and sit back. The plane was on its own for the first few seconds and then I took over. I was surprised at the smoothness—even smoother than a steam catapult launch from an aircraft carrier.

After its ZELL test program had been completed, this F-104G went into service in Germany.

RF-104G: The RF-104G was the only model produced as a dedicated photographic reconnaissance aircraft.

Two Aspide 1A AAMs on an Italian F-104S.
Lockheed via Campbell Archives

View of an F-104G (USAF 63-13240) as it banks left to show its underneath to good advantage. Out of the total of 2,578 *Starfighters built, 1,122 F-104Gs were produced—more than forty percent of the total.* Lockheed via Campbell Archives

A Lockheed-built F-104G in USAF markings prior to delivery to the Luftwaffe. General Electric

An F-104G in USAF markings during a practice sortie by a pilot of the 69th Tactical Fighter Training Squadron (TFTS) flying out of Nellis, AFB, Nevada, circa 1980. Note last two digits in its USAF serial number— six and nine, emphasizing its association with the 69th TFTS. USAF via Campbell Archives

A very shiny F-104G of the 69th TFTS on the ramp at Nellis AFB, Nevada, circa 1980.

Indeed, beauty is in the eyes of the beholder. William Spidle via Gary James Collection

The German and Dutch air forces received a total of 189 of these unarmed tactical photo-recce Starfighters. Fokker (the North Group) produced and delivered 119; Fiat (Italian Group), thirty; and Lockheed, forty.

The RF-104G used by the Dutch air force employed a ventral camera pack externally, while the German air force F-104G used three KS-67A cameras internally. A large number of RF-104Gs were later brought up to F-104G standard—that is, their photo equipment was removed and they became fully armed, all-weather, multi-role fighters.

TF-104G: Lockheed built 220 TF-104Gs in six versions recognized by the suffix letters C, D, E, F, G, and H after its Model 583 classification number. This amount includes forty-eight TF-104Gs with subassemblies built by Lockheed's European allies.

Lockheed kept one model 583D TF-104G airplane for a time to serve as a

demonstrator. It carried civil registration number N104L and was nicknamed *Free World Defender.* It was the TF-104G in which Jacqueline Cochran set her three world speed records. The airplane was later delivered to the Dutch air force as serial number D-5702.

TF-104Gs have served four countries: Germany, Belgium, the Netherlands, and Italy. Two former Luftwaffe TF-104Gs were obtained by NASA in July 1975 (registration numbers N824NA and N825NA). In foreign service, TF-104Gs were fully combat capable.

F-104J: Based on the F-104G, the F-104J (J for Japan) Starfighter was produced to serve the Japan Air Self-Defense Force as an all-weather interceptor, period.

Lockheed built three F-104Js. Mitsubishi assembled twenty-nine from Lockheed-built components, then manufactured 178 in two groups. The first Lockheed-produced F-104J made its maiden flight on 30 June 1961. F-104Js came with Japanese-built J79-IHI-11A turbojet engines, equal to General Electric J79-GE-11A turbojet engines. Japan assembled its first F-104Js in March 1962, its first Mitsubishi-built group through March 1965, and the last Mitsubishi-built group through 1967.

Previous page
A Lockheed-built TF-104G (USAF 61-3081) in USAF colors before its delivery to the Luftwaffe. Lockheed via Campbell Archives

An F-104G at an unknown location in USAF markings. Peter Wilson via Gary James Collection

Fine study of F-104G's tail group; the vertical fin of the G model had twenty-five percent more area than those of the A and C models for improved stability. Peter Wilson via Gary James Collection

CF-104: Powered by the Canadian-built J79-OEL-7 turbojet engine, the CF-104 (formerly CF-111 as first designated by the Royal Canadian Air Force or CL-90 as designated by Canadair) is similar to the F-104G. It served as a single-seat, all-weather, multi-role fighter.

Canadair built 200 CF-104 aircraft under a contract from the Canadian government that was awarded on 24 July 1959. The CF-104s were unique because they retained the removable in-flight refueling probe and drogue system used by USAF F-104C/D aircraft. Moreover, they could be fitted with ventral photo-recce camera pods à la Dutch air force RF-104Gs.

Lockheed flight-tested the first Canadair CF-104 on 26 May 1961 at Palmdale, California, after its arrival there from Canadair's assembly facility. A number of former Royal Canadian Air Force CF-104s and CF-104Ds (discussed below) went into service with Denmark and Norway, but only after their

Luftwaffe F-104G 63-13243 retains US Air Force markings while training future German air force pilots in the United States. External wingtip and underwing fuel tanks increased the G's maximum range without aerial refueling to 1,630mi. Peter Wilson via Gary James Collection

Previous page
Like the single-seat F-104G, the tandem-seat TF-104G carried the F15A NASARR system, and full operational equipment to make it a complete weapon system. Peter Wilson via Gary James Collection

Initially retained by Lockheed as a demonstrator with civil registration number N104L, this was the TF-104G Toni LeVier flew to Mach 2 to become the world's fastest school girl. It was also used by Jacqueline

Cochran to set world's records. In May 1965, it was delivered to the Dutch air force and given serial D-5702. Charles E. Stewart via Gary James Collection

CF-104D (104805) of No. 421 Red Indian *Squadron at RAF Mildenhall, Great Britain,*

circa 1983, shows how beautiful an airplane can be. Paul Biglow via Gary James Collection

F-104J 63-5019 at Mojave Airport, California, circa 1989. The J model was structurally similar to the G model but served as an all-weather interceptor. Charles E. Stewart via Gary James Collection

F-104S 36-01 of 36° Stormo at RAF Waddington, circa 1990. With R21G radar and two underwing AIM-7 Sparrow or two AIM-9 Sidewinder air-to-air missiles, the S model was an excellent interceptor. Paul Biglow via Gary James Collection

Luftwaffe F-104Gs were single-seat, multi-role, all-weather fighters powered by 15,600lb thrust (with afterburning) GE J79-GE-11A engines. F-104G 26-80 is shown. Charles E. Stewart via Gary James Collection

TF-104G 4-913 of the Turkish air force. Turkey got four two-seat TF-104Gs. Charles E. Stewart via Gary James Collection

modification program to bring them up to close standard with the F-104G variant.

CF-104D: Originally designated CF-113 by the Royal Canadian Air Force, the CF-104D was similar to the TF-104G. Lockheed built thirty-eight of these two-seat trainers for the Canadians. With some different equipment, the last sixteen CF-104D aircraft were delivered as CF-104D Mk IIs. Like the CF-104, the CF-104D and CF-104D Mk II aircraft were powered by the Canadian-built J79-OEL-7 turbojet engine.

On 18 May 1970, CF-104 and CF-104D aircraft received new serial numbers. Originally 12701 through 12900 (CF-104) and 12631 through 12668 (CF-104D), the new numbers were 104701 to 104900 and 104701 to 104738, respectively. The Lockheed-built F-104A pattern aircraft 12700 was renumbered 104700 at the same time.

F-104G 25-50 of JBG 34 at Memmingen, Germany, all decked out for the group's twenty-fifth anniversary of flying the F-104. Arnold Booy via Gary James Collection

F-104G 20-37 in natural-metal dress. Luftwaffe F-104s have worn various color schemes, but the standard for many years were the gray and green splinter pattern with light gray undersides. Arnold Booy via Gary James Collection

F-104G of 3° Stormo at Villafranca-Verona, Italy, circa 1989. The Italian air force is by far the largest current user of the F-104, the *majority being F-104Ss.* Paul Biglow via Gary James Collection

F-104G Specifications

Crew	One
Wingspan	21.94ft (without wingtip fuel tanks)
Wing area	196.10sq-ft
Length	54.77ft
Height	13.60ft
Empty weight	13,995lb
Gross weight	29,040lb
Maximum speed	Mach 2.20
Armament	One 20mm M61A1 Vulcan cannon; two AIM-9 Sidewinder missiles; various other tactical nuclear and conventional ordnance
Powerplant	One General Electric J79-GE-11A or foreign-built equivalent
Number built	1,122

F-104S Specifications

Crew	One
Wingspan	21.11ft (without wingtip fuel tanks)
Wing area	195.90sq-ft
Length	54.90ft
Height	13.60ft
Empty weight	14,900lb
Gross weight	31,000lb
Maximum speed	Mach 2.30
Armament	One 20mm M61A1 Vulcan cannon; two AIM-7 Sparrow and two AIM-9 Sidewinder missiles; various other tactical nuclear and conventional ordnance
Powerplant	One General Electric J79-GE-19
Number built	245

Chapter 8

USAF NF-104A and NASA F-104N Starfighters

NF-104A

For the purpose of training candidate astronauts, the USAF Test Pilot School at Edwards AFB, California, needed several trainer aircraft to simulate the training that was ordinarily provided by the trio of North American X-15 aerospace planes, but at a lower operating cost.

Since the high-performance F-104 Starfighter was easily modified to fill the aerospace-trainer role, Lockheed was awarded a contract by the USAF Air Research and Development Command in 1962 authorizing it to modify three F-104A aircraft (serial numbers 56-756, -760, and -762) into the Aerospace Trainer Aircraft configuration, designated NF-104A. These three A-model F-104s were taken out of storage at Davis-Monthan AFB where they had been mothballed. Major changes included:

• Deletions of the original F-104A vertical fin (replaced with the larger fin used on the TF-104G), the AN/ARC-66 UHF radio, the M61A1 20mm Vulcan cannon, the AN/ASG-14T-1 fire control system, the data link provisions, the VOR (VHF omnidirectional range) radio, the ILS (instrument landing system), the missile auxiliaries, the AN/APX-35 IFF (identification, friend or foe) system, the braking parachute, the auxiliary wing-tip fuel tanks, the plastic nose cone, and the J79-GE-3A turbojet engine.

• Additions of the TF-104G vertical fin, a 4ft wingspan increase to 25.94ft, an electrically driven hydraulic pump, new batteries for high-altitude power, a metal nose cone, an AN/APX-46 IFF system, special instrumentation, a test nose boom with pitch and yaw vanes, a Collins 718 B-1 radio, a pressure tank for cockpit pressurization, modified engine air inlet shock half-cones, a reaction control system, hydrogen peroxide tanks, rocket motor fuel system, J79-GE-3B turbojet engine, and one Rocketdyne LR121/AR-2-NA-1 rocket motor, throttle controlled from 3,000 to 6,000lb thrust with about 105 seconds' burn time.

At a cost of $5,363,322, Lockheed modified the three F-104A aircraft into the NF-104A (TDN CL-586) configuration. The first NF-104A was delivered on 1 October 1963, the second on 26 October, and the third on 1 November.

On 15 November 1963, the first NF-104A established an unofficial world altitude record of 118,860ft; this mark was later exceeded when this same NF-104A reached 120,800ft on 6 December 1963 (both records for aircraft taking off under their own power from a runway).

The second NF-104A, with then school commandant Col. Charles E. (Chuck) Yeager piloting, went out of control and crashed on 10 December 1963; though badly burned on his face, Yeager survived the ordeal.

The third NF-104A, with Capt. Howard C. Thompson piloting, suffered an explosion at Mach 1.15 and 35,000ft in June 1971. Thompson was able to safely land the aircraft; but since the aircraft's rocket motor and half its rudder were gone, and because the program was about to end, it was retired. The number one NF-104A is currently mounted atop a pylon in front of the USAF Test Pilot School.

The number one and three NF-104A Aerospace Trainer Aircraft flew a total of 126 flights. The last flight occurred on 20 December 1971 to mark the official retirement of these unique Starfighters.

F-104N

Between August and October 1963, Lockheed delivered three single-seat F-104G Starfighters to NASA, which it designated F-104N (N for NASA) to serve as high-speed chase aircraft. Initially numbered 011, 012, and 013, the first two F-104Ns were renumbered N811NA and N812NA; 013 was lost on 8 June 1966 when it had a midair collision with the number two North American XB-70A Valkyrie during a General Electric-sponsored public-relations-photography flight. Joseph A. Walker, piloting the F-104N, was killed; USAF Maj. Carl S. Cross, copiloting the XB-70A, was killed; Alvin S. White, piloting the XB-70A, survived.

These three F-104Ns were the only purpose-built Starfighters that Lockheed produced for NASA—other NASA F-104Ns were transferred to it from the USAF.

NASA received the seventh service test YF-104A in August 1956. Originally numbered 018, later N818NA, it was operated by NASA until November 1975 and is now displayed at the National Air and Space Museum in Washington, D.C.

NASA received four other F-104Ns—two single-seat, two tandem-seat—NASA numbers N820NA, N824NA, N825NA, and N826NA. While N820NA and N824NA have been retired to the Air Force Flight Test Center Museum, NASA keeps two F-104Ns at its Ames/Dryden Flight Research Facility at Edwards AFB. These include the two-seat N825NA airplane, a TF-104G, which will be used in upcoming X-30 National Aero-Space Plane tests, and the single-seat N826NA airplane, an F-104G, for other NASA-related programs. These are the only Starfighters still in US service.

NF-104A number one zoom-climbing toward the unknown; its Rocketdyne rocket motor is at full thrust—6,000lb. USAF

115

The three original F-104Gs that were purpose-built for NASA as F-104Ns; NASA numbers 011, 012, and 013. NASA

NASA F-104N number two in its original NASA colors at Edwards AFB, circa 1966. USAF via Tom Rosquin

The last tandem-seat NASA F-104N on flight status is a TF-104G. NASA

Next page
The last single-seat NASA F-104N on flight status is an F-104G. NASA

NF-104A was on a high-altitude zoom climb mission on 10 December 1963 near Mojave, California, when Col. Chuck Yeager lost control of the aircraft. Yeager ejected and parachuted to safety. The aircraft was destroyed. The primary cause of the accident was nonrecovery from a spin that resulted from excessive angle of attack and lack of aircraft response. It later was determined that excessive angle of attack was not due to pilot input but a gyroscopic condition set up by the J79 engine spooling after shut-down for the rocket-powered zoom climb phase. USAF via Campbell Archives

The retired single-seat F-104N (N820NA) that currently resides at the Air Force Flight Test Center Museum at Edwards AFB, California. Charles E. Stewart via Gary James Collection

Chapter 9

Starfighters That Could Have Been

A number of Starfighter variants were proposed for domestic and foreign use. Although none were ordered into production, they are discussed below.

RF-104A: In November 1954, the Tactical Air Command moved toward procurement of a photographic reconnaissance version of the single-seat F-104A—the RF-104A. Lockheed's design was approved by the USAF in 1956. In January 1957, however, all development work on this unarmed version of the Starfighter ended and the eighteen RF-104As on initial order were canceled prior to the completion of the first example. Tactical Air Command had planned on having four RF-104A squadrons, but it decided that the forthcoming McDonnell RF-101 Voodoo, the RF-101C in particular, would better serve its need because of its longer range and heavier load carrying capabilities. The eighteen proposed RF-104As had been assigned USAF serial numbers 56-939 through 56-956 prior to cancellation.

TF-104A: The TF-104A was a proposed tandem-seat trainer version of the one-seat F-104A that was not to be armed. Since the USAF preferred the combat-capable two-seat F-104B, the noncombat-capable TF-104A was not produced.

RTF-104G1: This was a proposed all-weather day and night photographic reconnaissance derivative of the TF-104G for use by the Luftwaffe. It was to carry side-looking radar, cameras, and infrared equipment. The Luftwaffe selected the McDonnell Douglas RF-4E Phantom II instead, and the RTF-104G1 ended in the proposal stage.

F-104H: A projected single-seat export version of the F-104G but with simplified avionics, an optical gunsight, and deletion of the Autonetics F15A NASARR fire control system.

TF-104H: With the same specifications as above, but based on the two-seat TF-104G.

CL-1200 Lancer: The Lancer was a proposed export fighter with the basic F-104 fuselage, but with a shoulder-mounted wing and a new tail group, on which the stabilator was moved from atop the vertical fin to the bottom of the aft fuselage. It was to be powered by either the Pratt & Whitney F100-PW-100 or TF30-PW-100 turbofan engine. The Lancer, developed by Lockheed's famed Skunk Works, was to be capable of flying 1,700mph at 35,000ft and a projected gross weight of 17.5 tons. In November 1970, however, its main competition, the Northrop F-5E Tiger II, prevailed and development of the CL-1200 Lancer ended.

X-27 (CL-1600): In 1970, the Air Force wanted to procure a number of Lancers to use as high-performance-engine test aircraft. The USAF planned to buy at least one experimental Lancer, to be designated X-27. The proposed X-27 was similar to the CL-1200 but featured modified engine air inlets of rectangular shape. The X-27 program was terminated for lack of funds before any of the aircraft were built.

A number of other F-104 designs were proposed, but little information has been released about their purposes and configurations.

Lockheed's proposed TDN C-901 with variable-geometry canard foreplanes mounted atop fuselage, aft of cockpit, was similar to Italy's F-104S. Lockheed

In August 1970, Lockheed offered its TDN CL-1200 Lancer—a prosposed air superiority fighter—to Germany, the Netherlands, and other free-world nations. On 5 August 1970, designer Kelly Johnson said, "It will be superior in air-to-air combat to any known fighter." Another Skunk Works design (note logo on engine air inlet), the Lancer was to be powered by the J79-GE-19 turbojet engine of 17,900lb afterburning thrust. No orders were forthcoming, however, and the CL-1200 program was terminated; the Lancer lost out to Northrop's F5E Tiger II. Lockheed via Robert F. Dorr

Chapter 10

Starfighters in Action

While the Lockheed F-104 Starfighter had come close to combat action on a couple of occasions during its early USAF tenure, it had been reprieved both times. That postponement, however, came to an abrupt halt in April 1965 when the 479th Tactical Fighter Wing (TFW) was first ordered to send twenty-five of its single-seat F-104Cs to Da Nang Air Base in South Vietnam.

When first deployed, these F-104Cs flew MiG combat air patrol (MiGCAP) missions, armed with their single M61A1 20mm Vulcan cannons and four AIM-9 Sidewinder missiles. This action helped neutralize the threat of aerial strikes against South Vietnam from north of the demilitarized zone. Later, F-104 jocks were given the secondary mission of flying low-level close-support strikes against ground targets.

Following the 479th TFW's first deployment on 20 September 1965, Maj. Philip E. Smith attempted to relieve another pilot who had been flying MiGCAP on station over the Gulf of Tonkin in foul weather at night. His navigation system failed, and he was forced to lower his altitude in an attempt to find his references. Instead, he was spotted by a pair of MiGs and immediately jumped. He was shot down at low altitude over Hainan Island, but survived the ejection only to be captured and made a prisoner of war. Major Smith holds the undesired distinction of being the one and only F-104 pilot POW. He was held in China until his release in 1973.

On that very same night, two F-104Cs flying RESCAP (Rescue combat air patrol) for a couple of hours trying to locate Major Smith had a midair collision while returning to Da Nang Air Base. In one tragic night, one F-104 pilot was shot down and captured, two F-104 pilots were killed, and three Starfighters were destroyed. One week later, another F-104 pilot was killed when enemy anti-aircraft artillery hit and destroyed his F-104C.

After those four losses, the surviving 479th TFW F-104s rotated back to George AFB, California, in November 1965; the aircraft had flown 506 combat sorties, totaling 1,706.9 combat hours. But beginning in May 1966, the 479th's SEA (Southeast Asia) camouflaged F-104Cs began redeployment of all four 479th TFW squadrons, this time to Udorn Royal Thai Air Force Base in Thailand. And, by June 1967, every single F-104C of the 479th TFW was in action. Yet the zipper, as the Starfighter was called by its pilots was not in the war to knock out MiGs—even though everyone thought it would be the USAF's top gun MiG killer—but to pound the ground with 500lb, 750lb, and 1,000lb general-purpose bombs and even napalm.

In July 1967, because of its limited range and subordinate mission, the 479th's F-104Cs were rotated back to George AFB for the last time. In thirteen months, the 479th TFW's squadrons flew 2,269 combat sorties, totaling 8,820 combat hours.

Upon their return to the United States, the 479th TFW's F-104C/Ds started phasing out of regular USAF front-line service and were transferred to the Puerto Rico Air National Guard and its 198th TFS. For the Starfighter then, both the Vietnam War *and* its regular USAF career were over.

This F-104A was disassembled and crated for airlift via Douglas C-124 Globemaster to Taoyuan Air Base, Taiwan, from the United States to participate in Project Jonah Able— the Quemoy Crisis; these 83rd FIS Starfighters augmented Taiwan's air defense. The squadron was later replaced by 337th FIS F-104As. USAF via Robert F. Dorr

F-104Cs from the 476th TFS are shown flying between Hawaii and Guam on their way to Southeast Asia. Ray Holt via Warren Thompson

A Chinese guard watches over a 476th TFS F-104 at Kungkwan AB on Taiwan. Ray Holt via Warren Thompson

A 476th TFS Starfighter is parked beside 509th TFS F-102s at Da Nang AB in South Vietnam, 1965. Bob Donaldson via Warren Thompson

An F-104 from the 435th TFS en route to Southeast Asia in January 1966. Morgan Lilly via Warren Thompson

A table is set in front of a napalm-loaded F-104 in preparation for a 100th-mission celebration at Da Nang, September 1966. Mike Korte via Warren Thompson

Ben McAvoy, Lockheed technical representative, stands in an F-104 cockpit at Da Nang in October 1966. Mike Korte via Warren Thompson

Next page
The 479th TFW's F-104Cs parked on the ramp in 1968 at Udorn Royal Thai Air Force Base, Thailand. USAF via Robert F. Dorr

A pair of 479th TFW F-104Cs en route to their targets in North Vietnam in November *1966 with a pair of 750lb bombs each. USAF via Robert F. Dorr*

A 479th TFW F-104C-BC (before camouflage), parked on the ramp at Tan Son Nhut Air *Base, South Vietnam, in 1965. USAF via Robert F. Dorr*

USAF Maj. Philip E. Smith was the only F-104 pilot shot down and captured in the Vietnam War; he was held in China until his release in 1973. USAF via Robert F. Dorr

After its return from Southeast Asia, this F-104C became part of the Puerto Rico Air National Guard, assigned to the 198th TFS, 156th Tactical Fighter Group. USAF via Robert F. Dorr

Appendix A

Lockheed F-104 Production and Coproduction

Designation	Serial Number	Quantity	User
XF-104	53-7786/-7787	2	USAF
YF-104A	55-2955/-2971	17	USAF
F-104A-1	56-730/-736	7	USAF
F-104A-5	56-737/-747	11	USAF
F-104A-10	56-748/-763	16	USAF
F-104A-15	56-764/-788	25	USAF
F-104A-20	56-789/-825	37	USAF
F-104A-25	56-826/-877	52	USAF
F-104A-30	56-878/-882	5	USAF
F-104B-1	56-3719/-3724	6	USAF
F-104B-5	57-1294/-1302	9	USAF
F-104B-10	57-1303/-1311	9	USAF
F-104B-15	57-1312/-1313	2	USAF
F-104C-5	56-883/-938	56	USAF
F-104C-10	57-910/-930	21	USAF
F-104D-5	57-1314/-1320	7	USAF
F-104D-10	57-1321/-1328	8	USAF
F-104D-15	57-1329/-1334	6	USAF
F-104F	59-4994/-5023	30	Germany
CF-104D	12531/12668	28	Canada
F-104DJ	16-5001/-5020	20	Japan
TF-104G	61-3025/-3030	6	USAF (MAP)
TF-104G	61-12262/-12279	18	USAF (MAP)
TF-104G	63-12681/-12684	4	USAF (MAP)
TF-104G	65-9415	1	USAF (MAP)
TF-104G	61-3031	1	Germany (MSP)
TF-104G	N104L	1	Lockheed-owned
TF-104G	61-3032/-3084	53	Germany (MSP)
TF-104G	63-8452/-8462	11	Germany (MSP)
TF-104G	63-12685	1	Italy (MAP)
TF-104G	63-8463	1	Germany (MAP)
TF-104G	63-12686	1	Italy (MAP)
TF-104G	63-8464/-8465	2	Germany (MAP)
TF-104G	63-12687	1	Italy (MAP)
TF-104G	63-8466	1	Germany (MAP)
TF-104G	63-12688	1	Italy (MAP)
TF-104G	63-8467	1	Germany (MSP)
TF-104G	63-12689	1	Italy (MAP)
TF-104G	63-8468	1	Germany (MSP)
TF-104G	63-12690	1	Italy (MAP)
TF-104G	63-8469	1	Germany (MSP)
TF-104G	63-12691/-12696	6	Italy (MAP)

Designation	Serial Number	Quantity	User
TF-104G	64-15104/-15106	3	Belgium (MSP)
TF-104G	D-5801/D-5813	13	Netherlands
TF-104G	D-5814/D-5817	4	Netherlands (coproduced)
TF-104G	KF201/KF232	32	Germany
TF-104G	66-13622/-13631	10	Germany
TF-104G	KE201/KE223	23	Germany (coproduced)
TF-104G	FC-04/FC-12	9	Belgium (coproduced)
TF-104G	583H-5201/5212	12	Italy (coproduced)[1]
F-104G	KF101/KF109	9	Germany
F-104G	63-13259	1	Germany
F-104G	63-13230/-13235	6	Germany
F-104G	KF117	1	Germany
F-104G	63-13236	1	Germany
F-104G	KF199	1	Germany
F-104G	63-13237/-13245	9	Germany
F-104G	KF129	1	Germany
F-104G	63-13246/-13258	13	Germany
F-104G	KF143/KF150	8	Germany
F-104G	683-2051[2]	0	
F-104G	KF101/KF109	9	Germany
F-104G	63-13260	1	Germany
F-104G	KF176/KF184	9	Germany
F-104G	63-13262	1	Germany
F-104G	KF186/KF189	4	Germany
F-104G	63-13263/-13265	3	Germany
F-104G	KF193	1	Germany
F-104G	63-13266/-13268	3	Germany
F-104G	MM6501	1	Italy (model aircraft)
F-104G	63-13274	1	Belgium (model aircraft)
F-104J	26-8501/-8503	3	Japan
F-104G	61-2601/-2623	23	Greece and Turkey (MAP)
RF-104G	61-2624	1	Greece (MAP)
RF-104G	61-2625/-2633	9	Norway (MAP)
RF-104G	62-12232/-12242	11	MAP
F-104N	811	1	NASA
RF-104G	62-12243/-12249	7	MAP

Designation	Serial Number	Quantity	User
F-104N	812	1	NASA
RF-104G	62-12250/-12253	4	MAP
F-104N	813	1	NASA

Designation	Serial Number	Quantity	User
RF-104G	62-12254/-12261	8	MAP
F-104G	62-12214/-12231	18	MAP

Notes:
[1]No Italian serial numbers were issued.
[2]Static structural-loads-test airframe.

Appendix B

Canadair CF/F-104 Production

Designation	Serial Number	Quantity	User	Designation	Serial Number	Quantity	User
CF-104	12701/12900	200	Canada	F-104G	63-13638/-13647	10	MAP
F-104G	62-12302/-12349	48	MAP	F-104G	64-17752/-17795	44	MAP
F-104G	62-12697/-12734	38	MAP				

Appendix C

Fiat F/RF-104G and F-104S Production

Designation	Serial Number	Quantity	User	Designation	Serial Number	Quantity	User
F-104G	MM6502/MM6599	98	Italy	F-104S	MM6660	1	Italy
F-104G	KC101	1	Germany	RF-104G	KC130/KC134	5	Germany
F-104G	MM6601	1	Italy	F-104G	D-6666/D-6671	6	Netherlands
F-104G	KC102	1	Germany	RF-104G	KC135/KC142	8	Germany
F-104G	MM6603	1	Italy	F-104G	D-6680/D-6685	6	Netherlands
F-104G	KC103/KC106	4	Germany	RF-104G	KC143/KC150	8	Germany
F-104G	MM6608/MM6611	4	Italy	F-104G	D-6694/D-6700	7	Netherlands
F-104G	KC107/KC115	9	Germany	F-104S	MM6701/MM6850	150	Italy
RF-104G	KC116/KC125	10	Germany	F-104S		18	Turkey
F-104G	MM6631/MM6638	8	Italy	F-104S	MM6869/MM6883	15	Italy
RF-104G	KC126/KC129	4	Germany	F-104S		6	Turkey
F-104G	MM6643/MM6651	9	Italy	F-104S	MM6890	1	Italy
F-104G	D-6652/D-6657	6	Netherlands	F-104S		6	Turkey
F-104G	MM6658/MM6660	3	Italy	F-104S		39	Italy
F-104S	MM6658	1	Italy	F-104S		10	Turkey

Appendix D

Fokker F/RF-104G Production

Designation	Serial Number	Quantity	User	Designation	Serial Number	Quantity	User
F-104G	KG101	1	Germany	RF-104G	D-8117	1	Netherlands
F-104G	63-13269/-13270	2	Germany[1]	RF-104G	KG218	1	Germany
F-104G	KG104/KG106	3	Germany	RF-104G	D-8119	1	Netherlands
F-104G	63-13271/-13273	3	Germany[2]	F-104G	D-8120/D-8121	2	Netherlands
F-104G	KG110/KG112	3	Germany	RF-104G	KG222	1	Germany
F-104G	D-8013	1	Netherlands	RF-104G	D-8123	1	Netherlands
F-104G	KG114/KG120	7	Germany	RF-104G	KG224	1	Germany
F-104G	64-12746	1	Germany[3]	RF-104G	D-8125	1	Netherlands
F-104G	D-8022	1	Netherlands	RF-104G	KG226	1	Germany
F-104G	KG123/KG144	22	Germany	RF-104G	D-8127	1	Netherlands
F-104G	D-8045	1	Netherlands	RF-104G	KG228	1	Germany
F-104G	KG146	1	Germany	RF-104G	D-8129	1	Netherlands
F-104G	D-8047/D-8053	7	Netherlands	RF-104G	KG230	1	Germany
F-104G	KG154/KG155	2	Germany	RF-104G	D-8131	1	Netherlands
F-104G	63-13229	1	Germany[4]	RF-104G	KG232	1	Germany
F-104G	D-8057/D-8063	7	Netherlands	RF-104G	D-8133	1	Netherlands
F-104G	64-12749	1	Germany[5]	RF-104G	KG234	1	Germany
F-104G	D-8065/D-8066	2	Netherlands	RF-104G	D-8135	1	Netherlands
F-104G	64-12750/-12752	3	Germany[6]	RF-104G	KG236/KG237	2	Germany
F-104G	KG170	1	Germany	RF-104G	D-8138	1	Netherlands
F-104G	64-12753	1	Germany[7]	RF-104G	KG239/KG240	2	Germany
F-104G	KG172/KG176	5	Germany	RF-104G	D-8141	1	Netherlands
F-104G	64-12754	1	Germany[8]	RF-104G	KG242	1	Germany
F-104G	KG178/KG181	4	Germany	RF-104G	D-8143	1	Netherlands
F-104G	D-8082/D-8084	3	Netherlands	RF-104G	KG244	1	Germany
RF-104G	KG185/KG187	3	Germany	RF-104G	D-8145	1	Netherlands
F-104G	KG188	1	Germany	RF-104G	KG246	1	Germany
F-104G	D-8089/D-8091	3	Netherlands	RF-104G	D-8147	1	Netherlands
F-104G	KG192	1	Germany	RF-104G	KG248/KG261	14	Germany
F-104G	D-8093	1	Netherlands	F-104G	KG262	1	Germany
RF-104G	KG194/KG195	2	Germany	RF-104G	KG263/KG265	3	Germany
F-104G	KG196/KG197	2	Germany	F-104G	KG266	1	Germany
F-104G	D-8098/D-8099	2	Netherlands	RF-104G	KG267	1	Germany
F-104G	KG200	1	Germany	F-104G	KG268/KG270	3	Germany
RF-104G	D-8101	1	Netherlands	RF-104G	KG271	1	Germany
RF-104G	KG202	1	Germany	F-104G	KG272	1	Germany
RF-104G	D-8103	1	Netherlands	RF-104G	KG273/KG274	2	Germany
F-104G	D-8104/D-8105	2	Netherlands	F-104G	KG275	1	Germany
RF-104G	KG206	1	Germany	RF-104G	KG276	1	Germany
RF-104G	D-8107	1	Netherlands	F-104G	67-14893	1	Germany[9]
RF-104G	KG208	1	Germany	F-104G	KG278	1	Germany
F-104G	D-8109/D-8110	2	Netherlands	RF-104G	KG279/KG281	3	Germany
RF-104G	KG211	1	Germany	F-104G	KG282	1	Germany
RF-104G	D-8112	1	Netherlands	F-104G	63-13690	1	Germany[10]
RF-104G	KG213	1	Germany	F-104G	KG284/KG287	4	Germany
F-104G	D-8114/D-8115	2	Netherlands	F-104G	63-13691	1	Germany[11]
RF-104G	KG216	1	Germany	F-104G	KG289/KG290	2	Germany

Designation	Serial Number	Quantity	User	Designation	Serial Number	Quantity	User
RF-104G	67-14890/-14891	2	Germany[12]	F-104G	D-8272/D-8273	2	Netherlands
F-104G	KG293/KG295	3	Germany	RF-104G	KG374	1	Germany
F-104G	63-13261	1	Germany[13]	F-104G	KG375	1	Germany
F-104G	KG297/KG303	7	Germany	RF-104G	KG376	1	Germany
RF-104G	67-14890	1	Germany[14]	F-104G	KG377/KG378	2	Germany
RF-104G	KG305/KG306	2	Germany	F-104G	D-8279/D-8283	5	Netherlands
F-104G	KG307	1	Germany	F-104G	KG384/KG385	2	Germany
RF-104G	KG308/KG311	4	Germany	F-104G	D-8286	1	Netherlands
F-104G	KG312	1	Germany	F-104G	KG387	1	Germany
RF-104G	KG313/KG315	3	Germany	F-104G	D-8288	1	Netherlands
F-104G	KG316	1	Germany	F-104G	KG389/KG392	4	Germany
RF-104G	KG317/KG319	3	Germany	F-104G	D-8293/D-8294	2	Netherlands
F-104G	KG320	1	Germany	F-104G	KG395/KG396	2	Germany
RF-104G	KG321/KG323	3	Germany	F-104G	D-8297	1	Netherlands
F-104G	KG324	1	Germany	F-104G	KG398/D399	2	Germany
RF-104G	KG325/KG327	3	Germany	F-104G	D-8300	1	Netherlands
F-104G	KG328	1	Germany	F-104G	KG401/KG403	3	Germany
RF-104G	KG329/KG330	2	Germany	F-104G	D-8304	1	Netherlands
F-104G	KG331	1	Germany	F-104G	KG405/KG407	3	Germany
RF-104G	KG332/KG333	2	Germany	F-104G	D-8308	1	Netherlands
F-104G	KG334	1	Germany	F-104G	KG409/KG410	2	Germany
RF-104G	KG335/KG336	2	Germany	F-104G	D-8311/D-8312	2	Netherlands
F-104G	KG337	1	Germany	F-104G	KG413/KG417	5	Germany
RF-104G	KG338/KG342	5	Germany	F-104G	D-8318/D-8319	2	Netherlands
F-104G	D-8243/D-8245	3	Netherlands	F-104G	KG420/KG423	4	Germany
RF-104G	KG346/KG349	4	Germany	F-104G	D-8324/D-8326	3	Netherlands
F-104G	KG350	1	Germany	F-104G	KG427/KG430	4	Germany
RF-104G	KG351/KG355	5	Germany	F-104G	D-8331/D-8332	2	Netherlands
F-104G	D-8256/D-8260	5	Netherlands	F-104G	KG433/KG435	3	Germany
RF-104G	KG361/KG362	2	Germany	F-104G	D-8336/D-8338	3	Netherlands
F-104G	KG363	1	Germany	F-104G	KG439/KG440	2	Germany
RF-104G	KG364/KG365	2	Germany	F-104G	D-8341/D-8343	3	Netherlands
F-104G	D-8266/D-8268	3	Netherlands	F-104G	KG444/KG450	7	Germany
RF-104G	KG369/KG371	3	Germany				

Notes:

[1]Reissued KG102/KG103 serial numbers.
[2]Reissued KG107/KG109 serial numbers.
[3]Reissued KG121 serial number.
[4]Reissued KG156 serial number.
[5]Reissued KG157 serial number.
[6]Reissued KG158/KG160 serial numbers.
[7]Reissued KG171 serial number.
[8]Reissued KG177 serial number.
[9]Reissued KG277 serial number.
[10]Reissued KG283 serial number.
[11]Reissued KG288 serial number.
[12]Reissued KG291/KG292 serial numbers.
[13]Reissued KG296 serial number.
[14]Reissued KG304 serial number.

Appendix E

MBB F-104G Production

Designation	Serial Number	Quantity	User
F-104G	2641/2654	14	Germany
F-104G	2655/2690	36	Germany

Appendix F

Messerschmitt F-104G Production

Designation	Serial Number	Quantity	User	Designation	Serial Number	Quantity	User
F-104G	64-12745	1	Germany	F-104G	KE340/KE397	58	Germany
F-104G	KE302/KE306	5	Germany	F-104G	64-12747	1	Germany
F-104G	67-14888	1	Germany	F-104G	KE399/KE419	21	Germany
F-104G	KE308/KE314	7	Germany	F-104G	66-13524	1	Germany
F-104G	67-14889	1	Germany	F-104G	KE421/KE431	11	Germany
F-104G	KE316/KE322	7	Germany	F-104G	66-13525/67-14885	2	Germany
F-104G	67-14886	1	Germany	F-104G	KE434/KE476	43	Germany
F-104G	KE324/KE338	15	Germany	F-104G	63-13526	1	Germany
F-104G	64-12748	1	Germany	F-104G	KE478/KE510	33	Germany

Appendix G

Mitsubishi F-104J Production

Designation	Serial Number	Quantity	User	Designation	Serial Number	Quantity	User
F-104J	26-8501/-8503	3	Japan[1]	F-104J	46-8564/-8658	95	Japan
F-104J	26-8504/-8507	4	Japan	F-104J	56-8659/-8680	22	Japan
F-104J	36-8508/-8563	56	Japan	F-104J	76-8681/-8710	30	Japan

Note:
[1]Built by Lockheed; assembled by Mitsubishi.

Appendix H

SABCA F-104G Production

Designation	Serial Number	Quantity	User	Designation	Serial Number	Quantity	User
F-104G	63-13275/-13278	4	Germany	F-104G	KH143/KH145	3	Germany
F-104G	KH106/KH115	10	Germany	F-104G	FX-67/FX-69	3	Belgium
F-104G	FX-1/FX-9	9	Belgium	F-104G	KH146/KH148	3	Germany
F-104G	KH116/KH117	2	Germany	F-104G	FX-70/FX-72	3	Belgium
F-104G	FX-10/FX-12	3	Belgium	F-104G	KH149/KH151	3	Germany
F-104G	KH118/KH119	2	Germany	F-104G	FX-73/FX-75	3	Belgium
F-104G	FX-13/FX-15	3	Belgium	F-104G	KH152/KH154	3	Germany
F-104G	KH120/KH122	3	Germany	F-104G	FX-76/FX-78	3	Belgium
F-104G	FX-16/FX-18	3	Belgium	F-104G	KH155/KH157	3	Germany
F-104G	KH123/KH125	3	Germany	F-104G	FX-79/FX-84	6	Belgium
F-104G	FX-19/FX-21	3	Belgium	F-104G	KH158/KH160	3	Germany
F-104G	KH126/KH128	3	Germany	F-104G	FX-85/FX-87	3	Belgium
F-104G	FX-22/FX-24	3	Belgium	F-104G	KH161/KH163	3	Germany
F-104G	KH-129/KH131	3	Germany	F-104G	FX-88/FX-90	3	Belgium
F-104G	FX-25/FX-27	3	Belgium	F-104G	KH164/KH166	3	Germany
F-104G	KH132/KH134	3	Germany	F-104G	FX-91/FX-93	3	Belgium
F-104G	FX-28/FX-30	3	Belgium	F-104G	KH167/KH169	3	Germany
F-104G	KH135/KH137	3	Germany	F-104G	FX-94/FX-96	3	Belgium
F-104G	FX-31/FX-36	6	Belgium	F-104G	KH170/KH172	3	Germany
F-104G	KH138/KH140	3	Germany	F-104G	FX-97/FX-99	3	Belgium
F-104G	FX-37/FX-39	3	Belgium	F-104G	KH173/KH175	3	Germany
F-104G	KH141/KH142	2	Germany	F-104G	FX-100	1	Belgium
F-104G	FX-27	1	Belgium	F-104G	KH176/KH188	13	Germany
F-104G	FX-40/FX-66	27	Belgium				

Appendix I

F-104 Production Summary

Primary Manufacturer	Model and Number Produced
Lockheed	XF-104, 2; YF-104A, 17; F-104A, 153; F-104B, 26; F-104C, 77; F-104D, 21; F-104DJ, 20; CF-104D, 38; F-104F, 30; F-104G, 139; RF-104G, 40; TF-104G (583C), 29; TF-104G (583D), 88; TF-104G (583E), 13; TF-104G (583F), 42; F-104J, 3; F-104N, 3; F-104S, 2[1] Total: 741
Lockheed Coproduction	TF-104G, (583E), 4; TF-104G (583F), 23; TF-104G (583G), 9; TF-104G (583H), 12 Total: 48

Primary Manufacturer	Model and Number Produced
Canadair	CF-104, 200; F-104G, 140 Total: 340
Fiat	F-104G, 164; RF-104G, 35; F-104S, 246 Total: 445
Fokker	F-104G, 231; RF-104G, 119 Total: 350
MBB	F-104G, 50
Messerschmitt	F-104G, 210
Mitsubishi	F-104J, 207
SABCA	F-104G, 188

GRAND TOTAL: 2,579

Note:

[1]Two Fiat-built F-104Gs (MM6658 and MM6660) modified to F-104S by Lockheed under Italian contract.

Appendix J

F-104 Turbojet Engines

Designation	Afterburning Thrust	User Aircraft
J65-B-3	No afterburner	XF-104 number one
J65-W-7	10,300lb	XF-104 numbers one and two
J79-GE-3	14,800lb	YF-104A and F-104A
J79-GE-3A	14,800lb	YF-104A, F-104A, and F-104B

Designation	Afterburning Thrust	User Aircraft
J79-GE-3B	14,800lb	F-104A and F-104B
J79-GE-7A	15,800lb	F-104C, F-104D, and F-104F
J79-GE-11A	15,800lb	F-104G, RF-104G, and TF-104G
J79-GE-19	17,900lb	F-104S and F-104S ASA

Note:

General Electric J79 turbojet engines for the F-104 were also coproduced in Belgium, Canada, Germany, Italy, and Japan.

Appendix K

XF-104 and YF-104A Disposition

Designation	Serial Number	Disposition
XF-104-1	53-7786	destroyed 11 July 1957 after crash
XF-104-2	53-7787	destroyed 14 April 1955 after crash
YF-104A-1	55-2955	fate unknown
YF-104A-2	55-2956	to QF-104A; fate unknown
YF-104A-3	55-2957	to QF-104A; fate unknown
YF-104A-4	55-2958	destroyed 15 February 1957 after crash
YF-104A-5	55-2959	used by General Electric in the 1950s as J79 engine testbed; fate unknown
YF-104A-6	55-2960	destroyed 3 November 1956 after crash
YF-104A-7	55-2961	to NASA in 1956 as N818NA; now on display at the National Air and Space Museum (NASM)
YF-104A-8	55-2962	destroyed 1 May 1957 after crash
YF-104A-9	55-2963	fate unknown

Designation	Serial Number	Disposition
YF-104A-10	55-2964	destroyed 2 November 1959 after crash
YF-104A-11	55-2965	to USAF Test Pilot School; fate unknown
YF-104A-12	55-2966	fate unknown
YF-104A-13	55-2967	preserved at USAF Academy at Colorado Springs, Colorado
YF-104A-14	55-2968	written off 6 May 1958; fate unknown (date also quoted as 3 May 1957)
YF-104A-15	55-2969	to QF-104A; written off 22 August 1957
YF-104A-16	55-2970	to F-104A; destroyed 27 May 1957 after crash
YF-104A-17	55-2971	to F-104A; to QF-104A; noted with 3205th Drone Squadron, September 1964; fate unknown

Note:
YF-104As were ordered and produced as service test air vehicles; however, the service test Y prefix was dropped as these aircraft were brought up to F-104A standard and/or modified to QF-104A target drone aircraft.

Appendix compiled by Robert F. Dorr

Appendix L

F-104 Records and Awards

The Lockheed F-104 Starfighter was famous for breaking all speed, time-to-climb, and altitude records (holding them at the same time); memorable to their record-setting pilots in making names for themselves in the record books; and noted for winning awards.

The F-104's high performance was first dramatized when it recaptured the world altitude record for the US on 7 May 1958, when USAF Maj. Howard C. Johnson reached an altitude of 91,249ft in a YF-104A at Edwards AFB, California. Nine days later, a YF-104A piloted by USAF Capt. Walter W. Irwin set a new world speed mark of 1,404.19mph over a 15-by-25km course at Edwards AFB.

In December 1958, flying from out of Naval Air Station Point Mugu, California, an F-104A set several time-to-climb world records ranging from 9,842 to 82,020ft. These are as follows: 3,000m in 41.35sec, 15,000m in 131.1sec (2min, 18.5sec); and 25,000m in 266.03sec (4min, 4.33sec).

On 14 December 1959, an F-104C raised the world altitude mark to 103,389ft (31,513m), thereby becoming the first airplane to take off on its own power and exceed the 100,000ft (30,480m) mark; time was 15min, 4.92sec.

The Robert J. Collier Trophy is the most prestigious award in American aviation. Presented annually for the "greatest achievement in aeronautics and astronautics in America" for the previous year, the Collier Trophy is presented by the National Aeronautic Association (NAA). The 1958 Collier Trophy was awarded to the USAF and the industry team responsible for the F-104 Starfighter: Clarence L. Johnson of Lockheed Aircraft Corporation, design of the airframe; Neil Burgess and Gerhard Neumann of the Flight Propulsion Division, General Electric Company, development of the J79 turbojet engine; USAF Maj. Howard C. Johnson, world landplane altitude record; and USAF Capt. Walter W. Irwin, world straightaway speed record.

On 15 November 1963, USAF Maj. Robert W. Smith piloted an NF-104A to an unofficial altitude record of 118,860ft by zoom-climbing from a high-speed run at 42,000ft. Smith experienced nearly complete loss of flight control above 90,000ft. On 6 December, he upped the mark to 120,800ft. The latter marked the highest altitude reached by any of the three NF-104A aircraft.

Civilian Speed Records

A pair of famed US civilian pilots, Jacqueline Cochran and Darryl Greenamyer, used two different versions of the Star-fighter to establish four speed records—three in 1964, one in 1977.

Flying a Lockheed-owned TF-104G demonstrator, which was later delivered to the Dutch air force, the late Jacqueline Cochran established three women's speed records on 11 May, 1 June, and 3 June 1964: 1,429.3mph over a 15-by-25km course, 1,303.18mph over a 100km closed circuit, and 1,127.4mph over a 500km closed course. She set innumerable speed and altitude records and was the first woman to crack Mach 2. On fifteen different occasions, she received the Harmon Trophy as outstanding woman flyer.

Piloting a former Canadian CF-104, which he assembled with help from American Jet Industries, Incorporated, in Van Nuys, California, Darryl Greenamyer set the current world speed record over a 3km course at restricted altitude at Mud Lake near Tonopah, Nevada, on 24 October 1977. He flew his specially modified F-104, which he named the *Red Baron*, to a speed of 988.26mph. Though he established this unofficial speed record, official recognition was not forthcoming because of a faulty recording instrument on the ground. He made a second attempt in February 1978 but the *Red Baron* crashed during his try. Greenamyer escaped and lived, but his F-104 was a total loss.

Bibliography

Books

Angelucci, Enzo, with Bowers, Peter M. *The American Fighter.* New York, NY: Orion Books, 1987.

Chant, Christopher. *Aircraft Armaments Recognition.* London, England: Ian Allan Ltd., 1989.

Davis, Larry. *Air War over Korea.* Carrollton, TX: Squadron/Signal Publications, Inc., 1982.

Drendel, Lou. *Century Series in Color.* Carrollton, TX: Squadron/Signal Publication, Inc., 1980.

Francillon, Rene J. *Lockheed Aircraft since 1913.* Annapolis, MD: Naval Institute Press, 1987.

Goldberg, Alfred, ed. *A History of the United States Air Force 1907–1957.* Princetown, NJ: Van Nostrand Co., Inc., 1957.

Jane's All the World's Aircraft, 1972–73. London, England: Jane's Yearbooks, 1972.

Kinzey, Bert. *F-104 Starfighter in Detail and Scale, Volume 38.* Blue Ridge Summit, PA: TAB/McGraw-Hill Books, 1991.

Knaack, Marcelle Size. *Post-World War II Fighters 1945–1973.* Washington, D.C.: US Government Printing Office, 1985.

Pace, Steve. *X-Fighters: USAF Experimental and Prototype Jet Fighters XP-59 to YF-23.* Osceola, WI: Motorbooks International Publishers and Wholesalers, 1991.

van Gent, C. J. *Fighter Meet.* Osceola, WI: Motorbooks International Publishers and Wholesalers, 1991.

Wagner, Ray. *American Combat Planes.* Garden City, NY: Doubleday and Company, Inc., 1982.

Periodical Articles

Alberts, Bob. "Flying the Zip '104." *Warplane,* August 1990.

Bashow, David L. "Star Warrior." *Wings,* June 1986.

Military Histories

History of the Air Force Flight Test Center: Bi-annual AFFTC History Office volumes, various sections, 1954–1972.

Index